Sunset
Kitchens
PLANNING & REMODELING

By the Editors of Sunset Books and Sunset Magazine

Country-fresh kitchen combines traditional charm with durable easy-care materials; the antique door hides a modern pantry. Design: Diane Johnson Design.

Lane Publishing Co. • Menlo Park, California

Acknowledgments

Our thanks to the many professionals in the kitchen remodeling and home improvement fields who shared their knowledge with our editors. We are particularly grateful to kitchen designer Beverly Wilson, who contributed the sample floor plans and devoted many hours to discussing the subject of design, and to L. E. Olstead of L. E. Wentz Co., General Contractors, who gave us the benefit of his expertise.

We also wish to thank Bob's Supply Co. Inc., House of Kitchens, The Kitchen Center, Major Lines of California, Oceanview Lighting & Home Accessories, and R & K Distributors.

Supervising Editor:
Barbara J. Braasch

Photo Editor:
Scott Fitzgerrell

Research & Text:
Scott Atkinson
Sudha Irwin

Photo Stylist:
JoAnn Masaoka

Design:
Joe di Chiarro

Illustrations:
Bill Oetinger
Mark Pechenik

Photographers: Jack McDowell: 1, 3, 7 bottom, 50, 51 bottom, 54 bottom, 55, 60 top, 64 bottom, 74, 75, 78, 79, 80. **Stephen Marley:** 7 top, 52, 73 right. **Tom Wyatt:** 2, 5, 6, 8, 9, 10, 11, 12, 13, 14, 15, 16, 49, 51 top, 53, 54 top, 56, 57, 59, 61, 62, 63, 64 top, 66, 67, 68, 69, 70, 71, 72, 73 left, 76, 77. **Tom Yee:** 58, 60 bottom, 65.

Cover: A new lease on life came to this kitchen when the owners remodeled for light, air, and convenience. Bright surfaces of laminate, synthetic marble, stainless steel, and tile combine with a corner greenhouse breakfast area in a graceful modern design. Photograph by Glenn Christiansen. Cover design by Lynne B. Morrall.

Sunset Books
   Editor, David E. Clark
   Managing Editor, Elizabeth L. Hogan

Fourth printing November 1986

Coordinated cabinets, counters, and sunny bay window combine for an all-new look and feeling. Surfaces are durable and easy to care for; recessed light puts illumination where it's needed. Design: Rick Sambol.

New skylight and raised ceiling provide daylight and improved ventilation. Counter design integrates cooking and planning areas. Architect: Robert Wylie.

Contents

Kitchen Makeovers   4

Planning Guidelines   16

Design Ideas   48

Remodeling Basics   80

Index   128

Compact urban kitchen uses light colors and a large green-house window to gain optimum light and visual expansion of space. Shutters maintain privacy from the busy city beyond. Architect: Fisher-Friedman Associates.

KITCHEN MAKEOVERS

Eight case histories · From facelifts to total transformations

Nothing is more helpful when you're first considering a remodeling project than to consult the experience of others. That's why we've chosen to begin this book with a series of factual accounts. Starting on page 6, you'll find eight full-color examples of successful kitchen remodeling. Projects range from moderate facelifts to several quite complete—and almost magical—transformations. Along the way you're likely to find one that will pique your curiosity, inspire your ambition, and, ideally, resemble the situation you face in planning or remodeling your own kitchen.

The following chapters lead you step by step through the design and remodeling process. "Planning Guidelines" (page 16) explores the design decisions you'll face, and includes a section on products and materials currently available. It also examines basic kitchen layouts, suggesting ways to alter and improve them. "Design Ideas" (page 48) contains more than 50 color photographs covering everything from floor plans to storage details.

Finally, "Remodeling Basics" (page 80) shows you in words and pictures how to dismantle and install everything from appliances to surfacing materials, walls, windows, and doors. There you'll find additional information on lighting fixtures, and overviews of your plumbing and electrical systems. Special features discuss kitchen safety, greenhouse windows, wall repairs, under-cabinet lighting, and energy conservation.

The book follows the logical development of a kitchen design and is divided into sections for easy reference. To begin, though, it's fun—and instructive—to see what others have done. Simply turn the page.

Many elements of good kitchen remodeling come together in this bright composition: well-defined work areas with lots of counter space, appropriate use of surface materials, a pleasant mix of natural and artificial light, and an open connection to the rest of the house. Architect: Michael D. Moyer.

A facelift was all it needed

The owners of this tidy kitchen decided to replace worn-out cabinets and appliances but leave the floor plan alone; they liked the layout, and major improvements could be made only at major expense. As the photos show, they got what they wanted: their familiar, comfortable kitchen wears a fresh new face; but now it's more inviting, and modern appliances and hardware make it work much better.

The final design, garbed in traditional styling, is restrained and elegant. Subtle touches distinguish the new kitchen: a slightly enlarged window enhances the room's overall feeling, and a coordinated use of fine materials and craftsmanship ties everything together.

Design: Diane Johnson Design.

New cabinetry combines traditional style with modern function. Cabinet doors conceal pull-out shelves; drawers glide on ball bearings. Soft blue tiles, both plain and decorated, complement the owners' china collection.

Bright new face (below) contrasts with the drab, outdated original (photos left). A window above the sink was enlarged to increase natural light and improve the view. Refaced and boxed in, the refrigerator presents a neater appearance. Crown molding complements the cabinetry and adds a finishing touch to the design.

Urbane renewal

Like the kitchen on the facing page, this compact room needed renewing. But here, the entire space is visible from an adjacent formal dining room so there was a need for maximum storage and minimum clutter in a clean, pleasing design that's always on view. The new kitchen provides all these things—and some spatial juggling makes it work much better than before.

The original kitchen had a short peninsula that served no particular purpose. In remodeling, this was cut off and its equivalent in counter space was added to the left of the ovens, which were shifted slightly to the right. Next to them, a built-in refrigerator replaces its more intrusive predecessor. New appliance garages were set into the cooktop wall, and rotary shelves were added to the corners of the U-shaped plan to make use of previously inaccessible space.

Cabinet doors resemble a raised-panel design but have flat surfaces for easy cleaning. A new greenhouse window increases daylight and allows for plant display. Vinyl parquet was used for the flooring that runs through both the kitchen and dining room—its resemblance to wood is uncanny.

Design: Custom Kitchens by John Wilkins.

New cooktop area concentrates storage in appliance garages set through the walls, and swing-out shelves that utilize space next to the dishwasher. All countertops are wood-trimmed synthetic marble, good for both wet and dry areas.

Clean lines of new cabinetry improve the view from the dining room. At left, a built-in refrigerator stands flush with the ovens and cabinets; before, all was a jumble (see above). A short counter next to the ovens provides needed preparation space; carousel shelves fit in below. A new pantry is located out of view, just to the right of the refrigerator.

Order out of chaos

The floor plans at right—before and after—tell this story best. Measuring only 10 feet square, the original kitchen sacrificed much-needed counter space and a coherent work triangle for the sake of an extra—largely pointless—door from the hallway (see upper plan). In remodeling, it made more sense to eliminate the door and restore order with room to work (see lower plan). As a bonus, the owners got a new breakfast nook; the adjacent powder room also gained a new lavatory.

The new kitchen has much greater—and more usable—counter space, and the work triangle is no longer cut apart by traffic flow. The new plan concentrates counter space near the cooktop; the old layout had none at all near the range, which stood alone between two doorways.

In the original kitchen, high windows to the southeast brought in welcome morning light, but as is often the case when there are windows in only one wall, lighting was uneven and the space uninviting. A new greenhouse window in the southwest wall now balances the daylight, adds a view, and creates a place for plants.

Materials and finishes greatly enhance the new kitchen. Colors are light and occasionally playful, helping to expand the space visually. In choosing the birch cabinetry, care was taken to provide continuous horizontal lines that carry the eye along; this gives the space a certain sweep that belies its diminutive size. Pink-hued marble tiles unify the backsplashes—an unexpected, distinctive touch. Their color is echoed in the back panels of the open cabinets.

Design: Osburn Design.

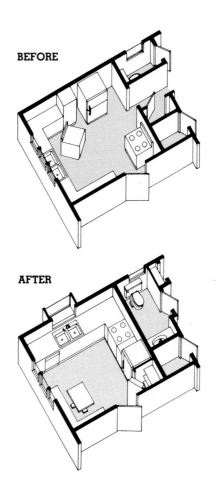

BEFORE

AFTER

New kitchen plan (right) contrasts sharply with the choppy layout of the original (above). New surfaces include parquet floor, birch cabinets, laminate countertops with bullnose birch edges, marble tile backsplashes, and laminate cabinet interiors. A new greenhouse window now balances daylight from the original windows, which were retained (see plans). Paper-towel holder and shelf above the cooktop hang on a horizontal support running around the room, and can be repositioned at will.

They took the walls away

Looking at the "after" photo of this serene, spacious kitchen, you'd hardly guess that it's only slightly larger than before. Only a little extra counter space was added (see plans), but two partition walls were removed with dramatic results. Kitchen, breakfast room, and utility room were all combined into a single bright space; yet each retains its original function and a sense of division from the others. Visually, though, each borrows space from its neighbors.

Crucial ingredients are the use of light-colored and transparent surfaces, and carefully controlled lines and planes that flow with minimal interruption. New plate glass windows in the breakfast room and a large butted-glass bay window beyond the sink affirm the indoor-outdoor relationship.

The simple geometric cabinets were given a sprayed auto-body finish; countertops and back-splashes are of complementary white tile. A large marble-topped pastry center links kitchen and utility area; a transparent cabinet above the rear counter divides the kitchen and breakfast rooms. Conveniently close to the cooktop is a new space-efficient pantry (see photo, page 77 right). Cork flooring adds a note of warmth, the yellow sink a splash of color.

To lend scale and sustain a hint of enclosure, the architect added a soffit around the kitchen. It repeats the lines of the counters below and houses the recessed lights that are keys to the overall lighting design. Crown molding is used where soffit meets ceiling—a nod to the traditional style of the rest of the house, and the only element that remains of the old kitchen in this elegantly transformed space.

Architect: Hiro Morimoto/Atelier Architects.

BEFORE

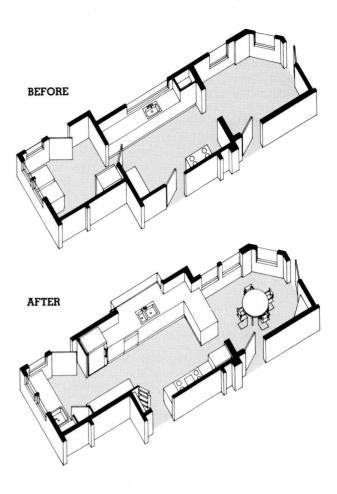

AFTER

Bright, open spaces (right) replace cramped, tired originals (above). Where a partition wall once stood, a transparent cabinet now invites your gaze through the kitchen into the breakfast room. A soffit encircling the kitchen preserves the room's integrity without constricting the visual space. New glazing emphasizes a connection with the garden outside.

Advantageous move

When owners and architect got together at the beginning of this project, they quickly realized that a reassessment of the house was in order. As the "before" plan shows, the original kitchen, while it served the formal dining room well enough, was completely detached from the large family room—awkward for a family with two children.

Their decision to move the kitchen to the family room revitalized both spaces with one stroke. Now, the kitchen-family room is the heart of the home, the new kitchen is as close as ever to the dining room, and a den—a quiet retreat for adults—is newly created on the site of the old kitchen. There's also a clear distinc-

tion between the formal and informal zones in the house. The kitchen really shines at mealtimes. Several cooks can work at once in the kitchen while onlookers lounge on nearby sofas, out of their way.

The relocated new kitchen features a large multipurpose peninsula, well-separated work areas, and a wealth of built-in storage. In addition, the architect provided a buffet and walk-in pantry by building out the walls just to the right of the hallway leading to the rest of the house. The cooktop sits in a new bay window that complements the existing bay window, now a place for the table and chairs.

Architect: William B. Remick.

Relocated kitchen (below) revitalizes the existing family room (right). Peninsula divider provides a desk, an eating bar, plenty of work space, and lots of storage. Behind it, the walls were moved out to make room for a new buffet, built-in ovens, and a walk-in pantry. The original fireplace is a linking element in the new design.

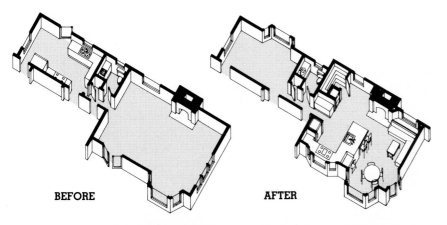

BEFORE   **AFTER**

Peninsula divider and the cooktop counter in a new bay window form two legs of an efficient work triangle (the refrigerator is just out of the picture, to right). Butcherblock makes up the countertops, with a tile insert in the wet area around the sink. Large drawers under the cooktop give easy access to cooking gear.

Up and out

Moving the far wall out 6 feet and annexing the attic above worked wonders in this formerly dark, cramped kitchen. Now there's a wonderful new ambience, room for an eating area, and greatly expanded counter space.

All was accomplished without major structural gymnastics: the extension is supported by diagonal braces running back to the existing foundation, and the new end wall is engineered to take up the outward thrust of the roof. An extra set of stairs to the basement was removed, making space for a much-needed desk and home office center.

The new kitchen layout employs an L-shaped plan, with the work triangle extended toward the desk where the cook spends much of her day. New windows in the end wall open up what was a nearly windowless wall, taking advantage of a favorable southern exposure. Enlarged windows to the west look out on an attractive deck. The ceiling is economical hemlock painted with a light translucent stain. Cabinets feature numerous large drawers, their faces made of recessed panels of beautiful rift-sawn oak set in simple oak frames.

Architect: William B. Remick.

BEFORE

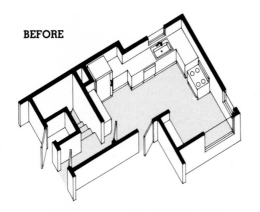

AFTER

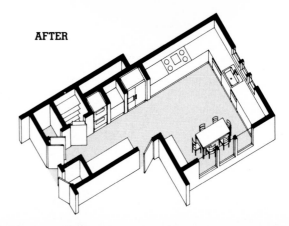

Moved-out wall and opened-up ceiling make a dramatic difference between old (above) and new (right). New design eliminated a window in the wall at left (it faced only the neighbors) and added new windows in the end wall, taking advantage of the raised ceiling and southern exposure. The remodeled floor plan almost doubles the counter space.

Patience rewarded

After years of saving magazine clippings, dreaming, and just plain putting up with their old, undersized corridor cooking space, the owners of this transformed kitchen finally got what they really wanted: a beautiful, light-filled arena for serious cooking and entertaining. They also gained lots of storage for the ever-growing collection of kitchenware that had threatened, like the contents of Fibber McGee's antediluvian closet, to burst forth from every cabinet and shelf.

Extra space and lots of light were added when a hip-roofed greenhouse was built in an 8-foot-wide notch in the original house plan; the diminutive dining room also grew, thanks to the addition of a generous bay window. Walls and roof are almost entirely glass, double-paned for energy conservation. A large sliding door gives access to the back yard.

The new floor plan is radically different. Now there are a large island and several separate work stations, including a baking center set against one wall. Extensive cabinetry ensures that it will be years—if ever—before Fibber's closet has any more rivals in this house.

Architect: William A. Churchill.

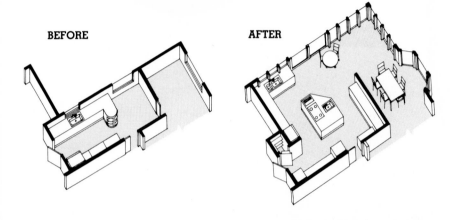

BEFORE

AFTER

Glazed addition fills in a notch in the original house (see plans). Large sliding glass door gives access to back yard. Double glazing was used throughout, for comfort and energy efficiency.

Greenhouse kitchen (above) is nearly twice the size of the old kitchen–breakfast nook combination—and infinitely more inviting than the original (right). The new layout features a baking center at rear, an island with several work stations, an L-shaped cleanup counter, and storage virtually everywhere.

Third time's a charm

At first glance, the contrast between the first two versions of this kitchen and the third is more than striking—it's almost unbelievable. But a closer look reveals the "bones" of the extraordinary results that sprang from such mundane beginnings.

The kitchen was remodeled twice. When the present owners moved in, the house, an older custom home, was pretty much a "fixer-upper." Funds were limited, so the goal was simply to make things more livable; remodeling was largely confined to the addition of new appliances and renewed surfaces. A fluorescent panel was added to the dimly lighted kitchen, and the peninsula was rebuilt to provide a desk-height surface.

Ten years later, the owners were ready to address the real problems: inadequate daylighting, insufficient storage, and inconvenient traffic flow. They were also anxious to bring out the home's latent architectural character. This became a major goal in what evolved into a whole-house remodeling scheme.

The result is a stunning success. Now the kitchen has ample daylight, thanks to its raised ceiling and large clerestories, and there's a balanced artificial-lighting plan that can generate light levels ranging from romantic to near-daylight intensity. New cabinets and the replacement of the peninsula with a large cooking island and pantry combination doubled storage. The island also corrects the traffic pattern, guiding people directly into kitchen or table areas; there's no longer an inconvenient detour around the peninsula when moving from one area to the other.

Architect: MLA/Architects.

New island replaces a peninsula, dividing kitchen-bound and table-bound traffic. A large gable clerestory (right) replaces the smaller window that once looked out on a neighbor's wall (photos above), creating space for a desk-height counter and banks of new cabinets. The sliding glass door was retained. Specially treated carpet runs throughout; the owners used it in the first remodeling and were pleased with its comfort and practicality.

BEFORE

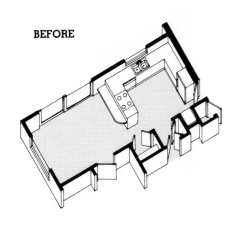

AFTER

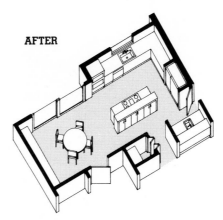

Complete transformation came from ordinary beginnings. First remodeling (far right) was a fix-up of the original (near right); the final version (below) brings out the home's real character. The ceiling was raised and the wall at the left was moved out. A new cooking island provides storage on both sides. The built-in refrigerator matches the cabinets; above it, a clerestory taps light from the new skylight over the entry hall beyond.

Planning pays off in this remodeled kitchen. Traffic through the kitchen to a new breakfast nook by-passes the main work area at lower left; an island further serves to route traffic away from the cook. Raised ceilings give an illusion of much greater space and allow for skylights and high storage. Architect: Steven Goldstein.

PLANNING GUIDELINES

Decision-making · Design · Floor plans · Products

Warm and earthy … sleek and sculptured … Whether your ideal kitchen contains a wood stove and open shelves or is the epitome of modern design, it's probably the most important room in the house, as well as the most expensive to equip. More elements—appliances, fixtures, plumbing, wiring, and furniture—fit into a given space in the kitchen than anywhere else in your home, and more time is spent there. Careful planning eliminates costly remodeling mistakes while you turn your dream kitchen into a working reality.

The scope of your remodeling project will be based on your priorities, available space, and budget. Once you've defined your present kitchen's problems and determined the extent of the remodeling project, you can turn to the exciting process of redesigning and furnishing your kitchen.

If you're simply replacing an appliance or adding sparkle to your kitchen with new countertops or floor covering, you'll want to explore the "Kitchen showcase" (pages 37–44); it offers suggestions about equipment and materials. When you're considering major remodeling such as moving a wall, you may want professional advice before settling on a new design. Perhaps you'll need help with the actual building. In any event, you'll need to have any major structural, plumbing, or electrical changes approved by your local building department. For more information, see pages 45–47.

This chapter discusses the entire remodeling process— from initial planning to final design, from evaluating your present kitchen to drawing floor plans for a new one. You can select and adapt the ideas that best apply to your own project.

A kitchen inventory

The success of any kitchen remodel depends on how well it suits your family. Who uses your kitchen? Is it a setting for family gatherings, or the private domain of a gourmet chef? To mold your kitchen in your family's image, you'll need to pinpoint some of its present deficiencies.

How many times have you complained about clutter on your counters or poor lighting over your stove, or simply cried in frustration, "I don't have enough space"? By making detailed notes and answering the questions on these pages (and any other questions that occur to you), you can assess your present kitchen.

Once you complete the kitchen inventory, review your notes and assign priorities to desired changes, additions, and improvements. Your priorities could be organized under "must have" and "would like" lists. You may later rearrange the priorities to better suit your budget, but these lists will become your most important planning and remodeling tool, even if you decide to hire professional design assistance.

Space allocation & layout. The three major kitchen elements (sink, stove, and refrigerator) form what kitchen designers call a work triangle; more trips are made around this triangle than to any other area of the kitchen. In the most efficient layout, the elements are placed so that the distance between any two of them (measured from center front to center front) is no less than 4 feet and no more than 6 to 9 feet, with the total of the triangle sides measuring no more than 26 feet. A greater distance means unnecessary walking; a shorter one means cramped work space.

Though it's not necessary for your kitchen to conform to this ideal triangle, checking into it is a good way to uncover any basic problems in layout. Next time you prepare a meal, observe how much walking you do between the sink, refrigerator, and stove as well as to the china cabinet and eating area. Do you have to walk around a closet to reach any of the points in the triangle? Is your wall oven conveniently located? If you share the kitchen with another cook, can both of you work comfortably without getting in each other's way?

Consider the layout of the room in relation to traffic. Do you have to walk through the kitchen to reach the family, dining, or laundry area? How many doors open *into* the kitchen? Do any of them interfere with the opening of an appliance or cabinet?

If a major traffic pattern intersects any leg of the work triangle, not only is it distracting for the cooks, undermining their efficiency, but it can also cause accidents. Efficient kitchen space allows cooks to work unhindered by pass-through traffic.

Work surfaces. Lack of counter space is a limitation in many kitchens. When you're preparing dinner, do your mixing bowls, hot pots, and salad greens vie for the modicum of space left on the counter beside an assembly of small appliances? Are dirty dinner plates often stacked where you would like to set clean dessert plates? Do you have a convenient work surface beside the refrigerator for unloading sacks of groceries?

And while you're analyzing your present work space, look at the condition of your countertop. Is it easy to keep clean? How does it wear around the range and sink? Do you have a heat-resistant surface by the range, a special surface for rolling cooky dough, or a sturdy top for chopping and mixing?

The height of a work surface should be comfortable for the cook. Is your counter so high that you're unconsciously straining to reach it, or so low that you're bending over to work?

Detailed notes on counter space should identify all problem areas—the need for additional space or more efficient use of available space, another surface treatment, or counters of a different height. Lack of counter space also points to another problem: lack of sufficient storage space.

Storage. One of the principles of kitchen storage is to provide maximum access for maximum use of equipment. To determine how well your storage space meets this requirement, take an inventory of all items stored in base and wall cabinets. Are items you use daily, such as spices, bowls, and utensils, conveniently located? Where do you keep lids, large pans, and other odd-size items? Are any cabinet shelves tall enough for large vases, jugs, and jars? Do you have pull-out drawers in deep base cabinets, lazy susans in corner ones? Is it easy to reach the top shelves of your wall cabinets? Do you need a pantry to store quantities of dry or packaged foods?

Sometimes solving the storage problem is simply a matter of reorganizing your present storage space for maximum effectiveness. But if you have a large family or use a variety of cooking and serving equipment, your present storage may well be inadequate as well as in need of better organization.

If you're fairly happy with the way your storage units function but dislike their appearance, you can refinish them. If you're planning to buy new appliances, though, you may need to replace your cabinetry—often dimensions of appliances differ.

Appliances. Outdated or worn appliances are one of the major reasons people choose to remodel. Changing an appliance, particularly if it's built in, may mean changing other elements around it. If you have no major complaints about your present appliances, perhaps they simply need a facelift. You can give them a new look with paint, wood, or plastic laminate.

- **Sink.** Tasks related to food—whether preparing or cleaning up—require the use of a sink. How convenient is your sink for each of these tasks? Is it large enough to hold big pans or mixing bowls? Does it have a garbage disposer? Would you prefer a sink with more compartments, or one made from a different material? Do you need an additional sink?

- **Range/oven/cooktop.** Another important appliance in your work triangle is the range or cooktop and oven. Does it have enough burners for your needs? Are the burners far enough apart to hold several large pots at the same time? If you have an electric cooktop, does it heat quickly? Do safety lights show that burners are on? Is your oven large and well insulated? Would you like to add a microwave or convection oven? Would you prefer a wall oven rather than one beneath the cooktop? List the features that you would choose in a new range or oven.

  Changing from gas to electricity or vice versa can be expensive unless you already have both utilities in your home. An electric range usually requires a separate 50-amp circuit.

- **Refrigerator/freezer.** The third point in your work triangle is the refrigerator. Is it large enough for your needs? Is it noisy? How often must you defrost? Is it energy efficient? Does the door hinge on the far side of the nearest counter? How easily can you open the crispers? Are drawers and shelves adjustable and easily removable for cleaning?

  Sometimes moving a refrigerator to a more convenient location can work wonders and save the cost of a new one. Unless plumbing lines interfere, such a move is not complicated.

- **Dishwasher.** If you already have this labor-saving device, consider how well it serves your needs. Is it large enough? Does it get your dishes clean? Are the shelves and racks convenient for your use? Is it too noisy or expensive to maintain? If you're thinking about buying a dishwasher, investigate these points as well as such features as energy-saving cycles and safety handles.

Ventilation. Few things are more unpleasant than having yesterday's cooking odors greet you as you walk through the front door. A good exhaust system rids a kitchen not only of cooking odors but of grease and heat as well. How efficient is your system?

Lighting. Working in a poorly lighted kitchen is not only fatiguing and depressing, but dangerous as well. Do you have ample natural and artificial lighting, or are your only light sources a small window and a ceiling fixture? Are you always working in your own shadow? Can you see into drawers? Is there a separate light source for the eating area?

  Make specific notes for each area of the kitchen in which you'd like better illumination. Enlarging a window or adding a skylight are excellent daytime solutions, but you still need to consider general and task lighting for the night.

Electrical outlets. Older homes usually do not have a sufficient number of electrical outlets to support the burgeoning collection of small appliances most of us own today. Does your kitchen have enough conveniently placed outlets? As you answer this question, think about any future appliance purchases you might make.

Heating & cooling. If your kitchen turns into a sauna in summer and you cling to the range in winter, your heating and cooling needs aren't being met. Check your present system. Before you make any changes, you'll need to know the location of ducts and outlets. If vents are located near the ceiling, do you have a fan to circulate the air? Is the air conditioning adequate? Do you have insulated coverings over windows or skylight to keep out winter's chill and summer's heat?

Walls & ceiling. A fresh coat of paint or some attractive wallpaper can give new life to any kitchen. If you're considering changing cabinetry, the walls and ceiling are likely to need new surface treatment. New countertops or floors may also mean a change in the color scheme. Look carefully at the condition of your surfaces. Do you like the color of your present paint or the pattern of your wallpaper? Are there cracks or chips that need fixing? Is the ceiling too high or too low?

Floors. When considering a change in the kitchen layout, pay attention to the floor. What is the condition of your flooring material? How easy is it to clean? After checking the surface appearance, note any sloping or uneven areas. These may indicate that the subflooring needs repair or reinforcement before the floor can be resurfaced (see page 114).

Appearance & style. The color and pattern of your walls, floor, and ceiling; the shape and design of your cabinets; the type of hardware and appliances—all of these elements contribute to the style of your kitchen. Functional aspects aside, do you like the way your kitchen looks? Is there a sense of harmony in the basic design? Make a list of what you would like to change.

Eating area. Whether your eating space is a counter with stools, a breakfast nook, or a table with chairs in one area of the kitchen, it's usually the place your family gathers. Is it used for activities other than meals? Do you have sufficient space for all activities? Is the lighting adequate? Is it out of the work triangle and traffic pattern? Do doors open *into* the space? Is it hot? Or drafty?

Special needs. If elderly or handicapped people use the kitchen, consider their needs. Does the kitchen have a low counter for sitting to chop vegetables or cut out cookies? Is there a stool to pull up by the range for stirring food? Are cooking tools and spices within easy reach? Are doorways wide enough for a wheelchair? Is the eating area set up for wheelchair access? What about the height of the sink? A few modifications in the cabinets and counters can make a kitchen accessible to a disabled person. Kitchen designers offer complete remodeling plans for a cook who uses a wheelchair.

Your present plan

Before you begin thinking about solutions for your kitchen's problems, it's a good idea to make scale drawings of the existing kitchen and any adjacent areas that you'd like to incorporate into a new design.

The process of measuring the kitchen elements and perimeters will increase your awareness of the existing space. Scale drawings also serve as a foundation for future design, and satisfy your local building department's permit requirements. (Depending on the extent of your remodeling plans, a floor plan of the existing kitchen, with proposed alterations, may need to be submitted to the building department before a permit can be issued.) And if you decide to consult a professional, you'll save money by providing these measurements and drawings.

These pages show you how to measure your kitchen, record those measurements, and draw a two-dimensional floor plan to scale. You'll also learn how to make elevation drawings of each kitchen wall.

Tools & materials

Listed below are some inexpensive tools and supplies that you'll need for measuring your kitchen and completing a drawing to scale. You can find these items at hardware, stationery, or art supply stores.

- Retractable steel measuring tape or carpenter's rule
- Ruler or T-square
- Triangle
- Compass
- Graph paper (four squares to an inch)
- Cardboard
- Tracing paper
- Masking tape
- Pencils
- Eraser
- Clipboard or pad with 8½ by 11-inch paper

Measuring your kitchen

Since even a fraction of an inch counts in fitting together kitchen elements, accuracy in measuring and recording measurements is vital. Before you begin, draw a rough sketch of the kitchen perimeters (including doors, windows, recesses, and projections) and any relevant adjacent areas. Make your sketch as large as the paper and record the dimensions directly on this sketch—when you sit down to draw your plans, you'll find that a labeled sketch is easier to use than a drawing with an accompanying list of measurements.

Write your first measurements in feet and inches.

Architects use feet and inches when drawing their plans, then enlarge the room plan and convert the measurements to inches when working with a kitchen designer. You may use your final plans (see page 36) to select appliances and cabinets from the "Kitchen showcase" starting on page 37; at that time, you too may prefer to convert your measurements to inches.

Measurements should be exact to ⅛ inch. Don't worry about showing those fractions in the scale drawing. When the work begins, you or your hired workers will be using the written measurements; the scale drawings will simply serve as maps.

Take care that the tape doesn't sag while you measure. If it proves difficult to keep taut, find a partner to help you or use a carpenter's rule. Double-check all dimensions.

Measuring for floor plans. A floor plan of your kitchen gives you a bird's-eye view of the layout of permanent fixtures, appliances, and furniture in the room. To make this two-dimensional drawing, you'll need to measure all the walls as well as the appliances, fixtures, and furnishings.

First measure each wall at counter height. Here's an example, using a hypothetical kitchen: Beginning at one corner, measure the distance from the corner to the outer edge of the window frame, from there to the opposite edge of the window frame, from the window frame to the cabinet, from one end of the cabinet to the other end, and from the cabinet to the corner. Note the locations of all electrical outlets and switches. After you finish measuring a wall, total all the figures; then take an overall measurement. The figures should match. If there is a difference, recheck your measurements.

Next, measure the fixtures and appliances along each wall. Note the depth and width of each appliance, adjacent counter area, and base and wall cabinet. If the appliance is freestanding, such as a refrigerator or range, measure the distance it extends into the room from the wall. Also note how far the doors open on all appliances. When measuring counter depth or width, be sure to include any trim, the backsplash, and any hardware or other part of the cabinet below that might project beyond the counter's edge.

Finally, make notes about the entry points of plumbing and gas lines, the direction the room's doors swing, and the depth and width of the range hood. Depending on the extent of your remodeling plans, you may also need to check the locations of load-bearing walls and partitions (see page 83). Record the dimensions of any tables, chairs, or desks that are permanent features in your kitchen.

Measuring for elevations. Elevations or scale drawings of each wall show the visual pattern created by all the elements against that wall. To create such drawings, you'll need to know the height and width of each element. You've already measured the width of the fixtures, appliances, windows, and doors on each wall; now you'll need to measure the height of these elements and the height of each wall. Follow a sequence similar to the one you used in measuring a wall's length. Remember to measure the kickspace (the space between the base cabinet and floor) and the thickness of the countertops. Add all the figures, and check the total against the overall floor-to-ceiling measurement. Also, note heights of hood, light fixtures, window trim, and valances.

Scale plans

The keys to drawing neat, readable floor plans and elevations are well-prepared sketches with accurate measurements; you also need a reasonable degree of skill at converting measurements to scale. Though architects generally use a scale of ¼ inch to 1 foot for their drawings, you may prefer working with ½ inch to 1 foot. A larger drawing not only is easier to compose (especially when you have to draw in all the fixtures, appliances, and cabinets) but it also offers more space for inserting dimensions.

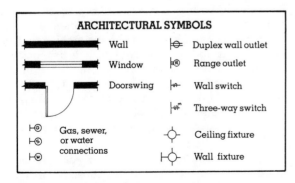

Drawing a floor plan. With masking tape, attach the corners of your graph paper to a smooth surface or drawing board. Use a ruler or T-square to draw horizontal lines, a triangle to draw vertical lines at right angles to horizontal lines, and a compass for drawing the doors' direction of swing.

Complete the floor plan, using your sketch as a model. To guide you, architectural symbols and a sample floor plan are shown below. Be sure to indicate the thickness of the walls and the shape of the sink (square or rectangular). Use dotted lines to show appliances in open positions. Finally, use a dotted line of another color to show the work triangle (see page 28).

How to draw elevations. Elevations are straight-on views of your kitchen walls (see page 30). Attach graph paper to your drawing surface; use one sheet of paper for each elevation or draw them all on the same sheet.

Keeping your sketch handy for reference, start by drawing the perimeter of each wall; then fill in the appropriate features of all of the elements against the wall. Be sure to indicate the location of appliance handles and cabinet hardware.

Existing floor plan

Poor planning makes this relatively spacious kitchen and breakfast area a difficult place in which to work. The counter that partially separates the breakfast and kitchen areas sticks out into the middle of what would be a straight traffic path from the back door to the hallway and dining room. The refrigerator extends too far into the passageway. Counter space is practically nonexistent, and the only storage area lies across the room from the sink and range. The division between the windows above the sink blocks the view. Two ceiling fixtures—one above the sink and one in the center of the room—are the only sources of artificial light in the kitchen.

For a comparison of the existing floor plan and the new plan, see page 36.

ARCHITECTURAL SYMBOLS

ARCHITECTURAL SYMBOLS

▬▬▬ Wall	⊨⊖ Duplex wall outlet
▬▬▬ Window	⊨® Range outlet
⌐▬ Doorswing	⊨ₛ Wall switch
	⊨ₛ³ Three-way switch
⊨⊚ ⊨⑤ ⊨ⓦ Gas, sewer, or water connections	○ Ceiling fixture
	⊢○⊣ Wall fixture

Architects and designers use a set of standard symbols to indicate certain features on floor plans; some of the most common ones are shown at left. It's a good idea to become familiar with these symbols, since you'll want to use them on your own plans, especially when you need to communicate with your building department, a contractor, or a professional designer.

Collecting your thoughts

Though every kitchen has the same basic elements—cabinets and countertops, appliances, and fixtures, walls, floor, and ceiling—it's the way you put those elements together, and the types you choose, that create a kitchen that works for you and becomes an expression of your style. Your kitchen design may appear to be dictated by the architecture of your house, but within limits you still have the flexibility to shape it into a more efficient and usable space.

Designing a new kitchen can seem like an overwhelming process unless it's broken into smaller, more manageable projects. By surveying your existing kitchen and making working drawings of its floor and walls, you've prepared the foundation for a new kitchen. Now you're ready to build on that foundation.

Begin by reviewing your list of priorities. Then let your imagination have free rein in creating a new design—this is the time to plan without restriction; you can consider actual limitations later. First, you'll want to sketch out an overall layout, thinking later about such details as storage, work surfaces, lighting, and decor. Even when you've decided on a workable plan, remain open to new ideas; you may need to make changes as you refine the design and consider the actual costs of materials and labor. Kitchen design is often a matter of tradeoffs, especially when you're faced with limited space—and budget.

Discussions on the following pages cover the individual elements of design: basic layouts, activity centers, work triangles, minimum clearances, traffic flow, and storage requirements. You'll also find material on line, shape, scale, color, texture, pattern, and light. If you're planning plumbing, wiring, or structural alterations, or improvements to heating and cooling systems, these changes will also be reflected in your final design.

Defining your style

A room's style is like a melody; its theme should provide structure, balance, and harmony. In a kitchen, style is determined by many factors—from architectural features to cabinets, appliances, fixtures, and accessories. To complement an existing kitchen or compose a new one, you'll want to consider the room's overall appearance as well as its individual elements.

Is your idea of the perfect kitchen a cozy room with warm wood surfaces, hanging plants, and comfortable table and chairs that invite family gatherings? Or do you prefer an easy-to-clean stark-white base of operations? Do you have a sense of satisfaction when you see bright, shining pans hanging in rows above your range? Do dishes parading across lengths of open shelving simply mean extra cleaning to you?

When you think of decorating style, be flexible. Don't limit your definition of style to such convenient labels as "country French" or "contemporary." Usually, a room is a combination of many styles.

Where to look for ideas. Since the kitchen is only one room in your house, stroll through the other areas, noting decorating features you especially like or dislike. Pay particular attention to rooms and hallways adjacent to the kitchen.

Next, study the photographs in the chapter on "Design Ideas," pages 48–79. They should at least prove inspiring, and you may find ideas you'd like to adapt to your own setting. Varied styles in appliances, fixtures, and cabinetry are also illustrated and described in the "Kitchen showcase" on pages 37–44.

To collect more ideas and learn more about products, visit stores and showrooms displaying kitchen appliances, cabinetry, light fixtures, wall coverings, and flooring materials. You can obtain catalogues, brochures, and color charts from these stores or directly from the manufacturers. Consumer and trade publications also offer helpful information on design, decor, and home improvement.

Start a notebook. As you accumulate notes, clippings, photographs, and brochures, organize your remodeling ideas in a notebook. Choose a binder with several divisions, or file your material in separate 9 by 12-inch envelopes. Organize by subjects, such as overall styles, layouts and plans, pleasing color combinations, appliances, cabinets and countertops, fixtures, lighting, and accessories. Then review your remodeling goals and adapt the categories to suit your project.

As your notebook becomes progressively thicker, note the decorating trends that most appeal to you. Perhaps a clean, geometric look with bold lines and bright colors pleases you more than a soft, more pastel appearance. Do you like the warmth of a kitchen with a low ceiling, or an airy feeling enhanced by a skylight?

You may also notice some design conflicts emerging. The bright wallpaper that looked so dramatic in a dining room might lose its appeal when brightly illuminated in your kitchen. Try to identify what you like about certain styles and attempt to incorporate those features in various elements of your design.

Planning constraints

Before you become involved in the process of transforming your existing kitchen into an ideal one, you'll need to consider a few facts about plumbing and wiring that may help you resolve layout decisions. You'll also find it helpful to read the information in the remodeling section (beginning on page 80) to familiarize yourself with the work that plumbing, wiring, and structural changes entail. Some alterations are simple and inexpensive; others are more complicated and costly.

If your house has a cement floor, you'll be limited in relocating or extending utility lines. For example, the only way to bring plumbing or wiring to a kitchen island may be to drill through the concrete—an expensive proposition, and one that may damage any heating pipes running through the slab. Where there's a wood subfloor, it's relatively easy to move supply lines.

If you're considering extensive rewiring or relocating major appliances, you'll have to gain access through the walls or floor. How much these changes cost will depend on how far you plan to move the fixtures and how easy it is to get to the utility lines. Separate local codes govern modifications in plumbing, gas, and electrical lines.

Generally, if you have flexible supply lines, you can move your sink a few inches without any problems. Your present supply line will probably also support a smaller second sink. If you're planning to move your sink within a few feet of the main soil stack (see page 90), you can simply extend the current supply and drain lines. Moving the sink any farther away will require more extensive work.

Relocating an electric range may be relatively simple if you presently have 120/240-volt wiring. You can usually move a gas range a couple of feet by stretching the flexible pipe from the gas shutoff valve, as long as the valve remains easily accessible in case of an emergency. One of the main considerations in moving a range or cooktop is the need to vent the exhaust system through an outside wall or the roof. The more direct the route of the vent duct, the less costly and more energy efficient the installation.

Usually, moving a heating or cooling unit is not too difficult; it all depends on the type of system. A heat register in the floor or kickspace can be moved by a change of ducting beneath the floor. Ducts for wall units can be rerouted through the wall.

If you're thinking of adding a new heating or cooling outlet in your kitchen, first determine whether your existing system can handle the additional load without loss of efficiency. If it can, try to locate the register in a spot where the ducting can be easily extended from your present system, and where you'll not be sacrificing precious wall space in your work area.

A COURSE IN KITCHEN SAFETY

No longer solely meal preparation centers, today's kitchens also function as dining, entertainment, hobby, and office areas. With so much time spent there, the need for ensuring kitchen safety has increased.

- Reduce fire potential by storing flammable items away from heat. Clean the entire cooking area frequently; grease buildup can be dangerous, yet it often goes unnoticed on concealed surfaces.

- Install a smoke detector between the kitchen and living areas, and keep a Class B:C fire extinguisher handy.

- If fire breaks out on a cooktop, cover the flames with a pot lid, apply baking soda or salt, or use the extinguisher. Never douse a grease fire with water and do not attempt to move a flaming pan. To smother fire in a broiler, turn off the heat and keep the oven door closed.

- Know the location of your main gas shutoff valve and how to operate it; gas is flowing when the handle or key is parallel to the inlet pipe, but shut off when the handle is perpendicular to the pipe. Store a wrench next to the valve for quick shutoff.

- Natural and LP gas are scented to alert you to leaks. For a major leak or service interruption, evacuate the house, turn off the main gas valve, and immediately call your utility company. For minor leaking caused by a blown-out pilot, ventilate the room thoroughly. Then relight the pilot according to the manufacturer's instructions, or call your utility company.

- Sparks can ignite gas—don't turn on electric switches, appliances, or other ignition sources if you suspect a leak.

- Use properly grounded outlets with adequate fuses. Don't overload your circuits (hot plugs are a sign of overloading).

- Check the condition of appliance cords, outlets, and switches; avoid using extension cords. Know where and how to shut off your kitchen's electrical circuits.

- Keep appliances away from water; never touch water while you're using them. Always unplug appliances for cleaning or repairs.

- Kitchens invite exploration by children, so be prepared. Lock up chemicals, and don't store harmful substances in empty food containers.

- Block electric sockets with safety plugs. Buy appliances with controls out of the reach of children. Keep knives and small appliances out of children's reach. And keep a first aid kit in the kitchen for quick treatment of burns and cuts.

Basic design principles

A successful kitchen fits your lifestyle, allowing you to work comfortably and efficiently. Kitchen designers recommend some basic guidelines for the design of such a kitchen. The perspective drawing on the facing page illustrates many of the major principles and suggests some minimum clearances. But your kitchen doesn't have to contain all of these ideal conditions to work well for you. You can bend or break any "rule" to fit your needs.

The sum of the parts

When you're planning your kitchen, it's helpful to divide the room according to the functions performed in different areas—cleanup, cooking, food storage, eating, menu planning, and so forth. Though all of these spaces are interrelated, it's easier to examine their design elements separately.

If you're considering where to use cheery wall tile, perhaps a sink backsplash is just the place. The hanging lamp you covet might prove inadequate to light a desk, but fit perfectly over a table and chairs.

Breaking your space into individual components requires some reshuffling of your idea notebook, but you'll end up with a more organized approach when you're ready to purchase equipment.

Design guidelines

The following guidelines lend assistance in determining adequate counter space, correct counter heights, and minimum clearances for maximum efficiency. They also present ideas on the most desirable arrangement for kitchen appliances and the best location for storage in each of the kitchen centers. Applying some of these basic principles will help turn your time in the kitchen from drudgery to delight.

As you consider these guidelines, you'll also need to establish a relationship between the kitchen and the rest of the house. Can you divert traffic out of what would be the perfect place for appliances or a long run of counters? Is there adequate aisle clearance for workers and those simply passing through?

- **Identify each work area.** In your planning, be sure each center is complete with needed appliances, adequate work surfaces, and storage for necessary tools and equipment.

- **Four centers are basic** to most kitchens: cleanup, cooking, preparation or mixing, and cooling or food storage. Other, more specialized, areas—a baking or serving center, for example—can increase kitchen efficiency. In addition, you may want to include a planning/work center or entertaining center with a second sink and under-cabinet refrigerator.

- **Locate the major appliances**—sink, range, and refrigerator—so that the resulting work triangle (see page 18) is out of the traffic pattern, with the sink and range placed 4 to 6 feet apart.

The space for each appliance varies, depending on make and model (see pages 37–42). For planning purposes, allow 36 inches for refrigerator or double-bowl sink, 24 inches for dishwasher or single-bowl sink, and 30 inches for range or built-in cooktop.

- **Plan heights of work surfaces** according to the heights of the cooks. A surface 3 inches below elbow height is suitable for most tasks; however, tasks that require downward force, such as chopping, mixing, or rolling dough, are more easily performed at a counter 6 or 7 inches below elbow level.

- **Allow sufficient counter space** for each task; the minimums are shown in the drawing on the facing page. If you're right-handed, allot the largest amount of counter space to the right of the sink and a lesser amount on the left. Reverse the configuration if you're left-handed. If kitchen space is limited, you can let different functions share a counter. When combining work surfaces, choose the larger of the two minimum dimensions and add 18 inches.

- **Store small appliances,** equipment, tools, and supplies near the area where they're used. (In the color photographs you'll see a number of ways appliance "garages" are used to add counter space and park small appliances.) You'll save steps if dishes are stored in the cleanup center where they are washed, for example. The cleanup area should also include storage for cleaning supplies, dry foods such as onions and potatoes, foods initially prepared at the sink, and the tools and pans needed to cook these foods.

- **Provide adequate clearance** in aisles and near eating areas. Between opposite work counters, allow at least 48 inches. Expand that clearance by an additional 6 to 16 inches if two or more people are likely to share the kitchen. If the dining table is near a passage, allow at least 32 inches for walking past a seated person. When your table is positioned away from passages, counters, or appliances, you'll only need 26 inches minimum clearance behind each seated person.

Don't forget to allow sufficient clearance for cabinets and front-opening appliances such as refrigerators, ranges, dishwashers, and trash compactors.

- **Place tall appliances or cabinets** on the ends of a run of counter to avoid interrupting the work flow. Doors should open out from the room, especially where they might conflict with the opening of a cabinet or an appliance.

- **As a safety measure,** a range is best positioned away from a window where a breeze might extinguish gas flames or where curtains might be easily ignited. For more safety information, see page 23.

KITCHEN PLANNING AT A GLANCE

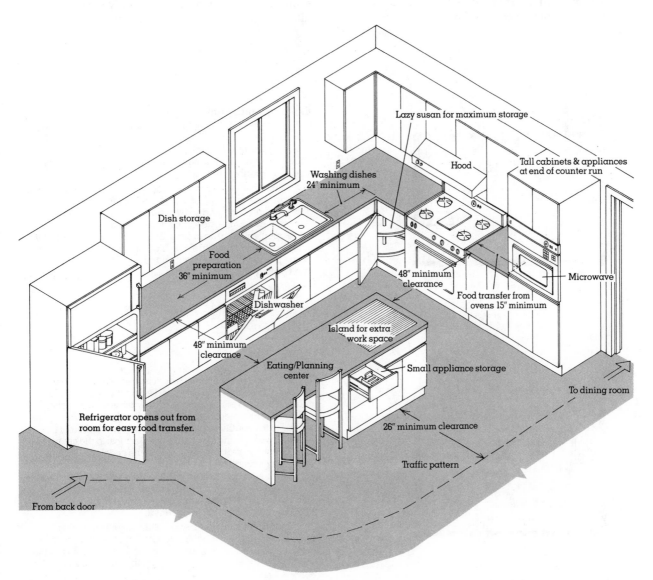

Lazy susan for maximum storage

Hood

Tall cabinets & appliances at end of counter run

Washing dishes 24" minimum

Dish storage

Food preparation 36" minimum

48" minimum clearance

Food transfer from ovens 15" minimum

Microwave

Dishwasher

Island for extra work space

48" minimum clearance

Small appliance storage

Eating/Planning center

To dining room

Refrigerator opens out from room for easy food transfer.

26" minimum clearance

Traffic pattern

From back door

Some kitchen design principles and suggested minimum clearances are illustrated above. The minimums are indicated only as an idea of the space that professionals feel works best; your kitchen can certainly differ.

- Major kitchen elements—sink, range, and refrigerator—form a work triangle. For efficiency, these three elements should be positioned so that the distance between any of them (measured from center front to center front) is at least 4 feet and no more than 9 feet. The sum of the triangle sides should be no more than 26 feet.

- The work triangle should be out of the traffic pattern. In the kitchen above, adding an island diverted the flow, allowing the cook to work without interference.

- Allow sufficient space between counters and near eating areas. You'll need at least 48 inches between opposite work counters and 26 inches minimum clearance behind each seated person.

- For best work flow, tall appliances or cabinets should be positioned at the ends of counters. Doors should open out from a room to avoid conflict with a cabinet or appliance opening.

- Allow sufficient clearance for cabinets and front-opening appliances. You'll need at least 20 inches in front of a dishwasher for loading.

- Adequate countertop space should be allowed for every task; some of the minimums are shown above.

Sample plans for a small kitchen

The sample plan on this page illustrates how one family transformed their kitchen within given space and budget constraints. Perhaps some of the ideas used for the rearrangement of space will be useful to you.

The existing floor plan is accompanied by two optional design changes. The first option is the more economical choice and includes only minor structural alterations; see page 21 for architectural symbols.

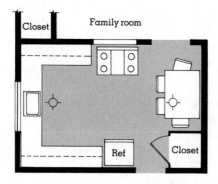

Existing small kitchen

High, narrow counters, lack of adequate work surface, poor lighting, and a crowded eating area are some of this kitchen's major problems. The range has no hood or fan, and the window above the sink stays shaded most of the time by the side of a neighbor's house.

Along with improved lighting, storage, and work space, the priorities call for all new appliances, including a downventing cooktop and two ovens—microwave and conventional. Since the family has three small children, a more open eating area is desirable. Some shelves and over-cabinet display areas are also high on the list. No space for expansion is available; slight changes in the wall between the family room and kitchen are possible.

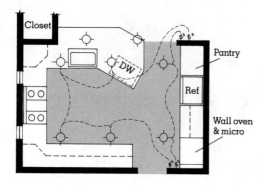

Option 1

The wall between the family room and the kitchen is partially removed. Replacing it, an angled peninsula with a wide countertop houses the sink and dishwasher on the kitchen side and serves as the eating area for the family room. The range is moved to the southwest wall and the window behind it is closed. Two long, narrow windows—almost to the ceiling—are cut into the wall on either side of the cooktop. A pantry, refrigerator, small menu-planning area, and wall ovens replace the old closet and dining table on the northeast wall. Moving the refrigerator to this wall makes the work triangle slightly larger, but allows open work space in the rest of the kitchen and creates a baking center.

Task lighting comes from under-cabinet fluorescent fixtures and four downlights overhanging the wall-mounted cabinets. The traffic area is illuminated by downlights; ceiling-mounted fixtures above the sink light the eating area.

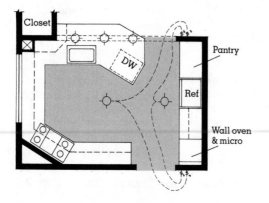

Option 2

To allow more counter space between the cooktop and sink while creating a more interesting design, the cooktop is placed at an angle between the south and west walls, parallel to the angle of the peninsula. Wall cabinets line the south and west walls. A corner cabinet or open shelves are added above the cooktop. The door opening to the dining room is widened to match the opening to the family room. This also provides elbow room near the wall ovens.

With ceiling opened, two skylights are added on the north wall; on the west wall, three clerestories follow the pitch of the roof, and a translucent, 6-foot horizontal window separates the counter and wall cabinets. In this raised-ceiling kitchen, downlights are replaced by globe fixtures that hang from tracks running along the roof peak and along a support beam over the eating counter.

Sample plans for a large kitchen

The kitchen on this page is a good example of two ways to improve a poor design—one in which traffic patterns are broken by several entries; and insufficient light and storage space make working a real chore.

Though the first option solves many problems, the second accomplishes this family's goals. The second option requires a higher budget and more substantial changes. See page 21 for architectural symbols.

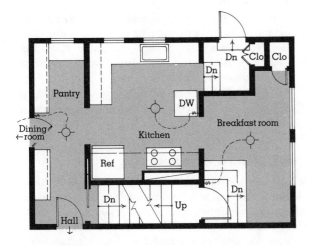

Existing large kitchen

This kitchen suffers from poor planning and useless partitions. The kitchen and breakfast room are broken up by steps from the outside and the front hall. The pantry and corner closets are small and not very useful. Narrow, insufficient counter space is annoying; there are no counters near the stove and refrigerator. High, viewless windows take up valuable storage space. The ceiling is lowered above the range, and lighting is inadequate.

Besides more counter space, better storage, and improved lighting, priorities include a new sink, dishwasher, microwave oven, range, and refrigerator; glass-fronted cabinets to display china; bookcases and a chair in the breakfast room. The breakfast room windows cannot be altered, and a second entry into the kitchen must be kept.

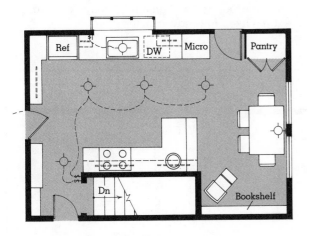

Option 1

All partition walls, including those enclosing the range and refrigerator, have been removed. The lowered ceiling above the range is eliminated. The floor level near the side entry has been raised and the door reversed. Entry into the breakfast area from the hallway is closed off; the steps are removed. A large greenhouse window over the sink replaces the small, high windows in the northwest wall.

New refrigerator, dishwasher, pantry, and wall ovens are installed along the northwest wall. The range is kept against the same wall to take advantage of an existing duct. A small sink added to the counter beside the range eliminates unnecessary steps while cooking.

To leave an open line of vision from the dining room to the breakfast area, no overhead cabinets are added above the peninsula. Bookshelves and a chaise are placed along the southeast wall. Task lighting comes from a downlight over the sink and under-cabinet lights above the range and sink area.

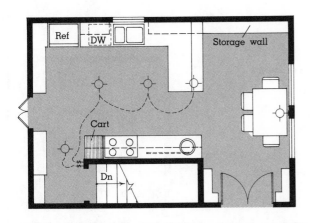

Option 2

The side entry along the northwest wall is closed and replaced by French doors (leading to a partially enclosed front yard) on the southeast wall. The peninsula is relocated on the opposite wall. Widened to 36 inches, it accommodates 24-inch-deep drawers facing the kitchen and 12-inch-deep cupboards in the breakfast area. A 12-inch-deep storage wall replaces the pantry.

Shifting the sink away from the refrigerator creates space for a dishwasher to its left. A standard window above the sink brings in natural light. The location of the range is changed to make room for an 18-inch pull-out cart with butcherblock top.

Design: Layout

An ideal floor plan eases the cook's work and enables others to enjoy the kitchen's warmth and fragrance without getting in the way. Though most kitchen layouts are similar to the basic ones shown in the illustrations below, you should let the shape of your room and your particular needs determine the final plan.

When space permits, don't hesitate to consider taking out walls or relocating or closing off a door or window. If the result is a more efficient and pleasant kitchen, it may be well worth the extra expense.

Begin by tracing the scale floor plan of your existing kitchen and any adjoining space you can "borrow." If you're considering removing or relocating walls, eliminate these existing partitions. Now try different arrangements on the tracing. As you experiment, set aside the plan you like, and start fresh with another tracing of the kitchen's perimeter in its future form.

Dividing your space

In looking at your available space, decide where you'd like to perform what activities. If a window offers a pleasant view, would you rather enjoy it while eating or while washing dishes? Would you like to cook or prepare food on an island or peninsula? Imagine all the possibilities and then draw circles on the plan to represent the locations of different work areas.

Consider major or minor structural changes that would increase your options for locating activity centers. If your present window offers only a view of a neighbor's wall, could you close it and open another wall or the roof for light and view? Such a change might allow you to place your cooktop beneath the existing window.

To help visualize how a proposed change will affect the room, create a mockup of the situation. Close a door, relocate a table, or set up an island made from boxes, and go through the motions of working with the new arrangement.

Concentrate only on overall space planning for now; you can work out the specifics of each work center later.

Positioning appliances

When you have a general idea of how you'd like to remodel the space in your new kitchen, focus your attention on locating appliances for each work center. Using actual dimensions if possible, make cardboard cutouts to scale of all major and minor appliances you'd like to use in your kitchen; cutouts should indicate the location of door handles. Move the cutouts around on your traced plan until you find an arrangement you like. Now draw it on the plan.

SAMPLE LAYOUTS & WORK TRIANGLES

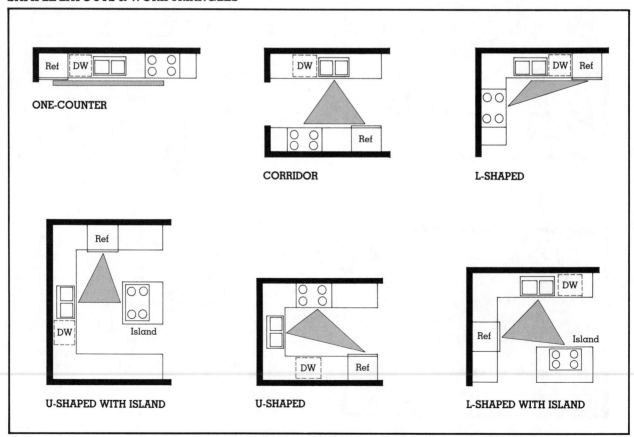

ONE-COUNTER

CORRIDOR

L-SHAPED

U-SHAPED WITH ISLAND

U-SHAPED

L-SHAPED WITH ISLAND

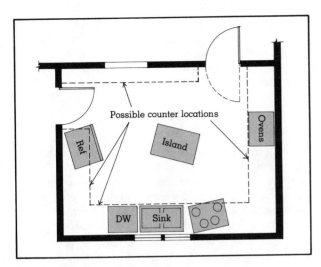

Positioning kitchen elements
To visualize possible layouts, make scale cutouts of major kitchen elements and move them around your traced plan for best positioning.

Begin with major appliances—sink, range, and refrigerator—that are used most frequently. For recommended distances between appliances, refer to the planning guidelines on page 25.

Once you've come up with one or two plans for major appliances, start positioning others. Place the dishwasher on one side of the sink, leaving at least 20 inches in front for room to load the machine. This loading requirement is particularly important if your sink is in a corner or on an adjacent counter at right angles to the dishwasher.

Do you want a microwave oven built into a wall, as part of a wall oven unit, or placed on a shelf above a counter? Because a microwave takes up valuable work space, it shouldn't be placed directly on a counter. If you plan to use it mainly for thawing frozen foods or heating leftovers, it can be located near the refrigerator; when it's used mostly for main dishes, consider placing it near the cooking or mixing center.

Blocking out work surfaces

Generally, countertops connect major appliances, providing necessary surfaces for food preparation and cleanup. Using the standard counter depth of 24 inches, sketch in the work areas on your plan. If space is limited, combine surfaces for different tasks. Match the longest surface with the most space-consuming chores. Add pull-out boards for additional work surfaces.

Outlining storage

Even though you'll be working out the details of storage when you draw wall plans or elevations, you need to outline general storage areas now.

The layout of appliances and the lengths of work surfaces affect storage possibilities. Any space beneath the counters that is not taken up by an appliance such as a dishwasher or trash compactor will be available for base cabinet or drawer storage. A garbage disposer limits storage beneath the sink; a drop-in cooktop offers additional storage underneath.

Think about the best positions for wall cabinets (usually 12 inches deep), and indicate them on the plan with a dotted line approximately halfway in from the line representing work surfaces. Modular base and wall cabinets come in 3-inch increments. Show any storage wall or walk-in pantry, too.

If your current plan doesn't give you enough storage and work area, try different configurations.

Locating eating areas

If you want an eating area in the kitchen, think about how you'll use it. For quick breakfasts or occasional meals, you might plan an eating counter on the outside of a peninsula or island; for regular meals, you'll probably want a separate table, placed away from main traffic and the functional part of the kitchen. Should you lack the room to allow clearance for individual chairs (see planning guidelines on page 24), consider fixed, upholstered seats. Adding a bay window or a greenhouse section can create more dining space.

Planning special work or hobby areas

A dining table or eating counter can double as an office/menu-planning center (especially if you include nearby storage areas) or can provide a place for children to do homework. But if your space permits, indicate on the plan where you'd like to sew or pay bills or enjoy other work or hobbies.

If there's a gourmet cook in your family, you might choose to add entertainment, baking, barbecuing, pasta-making, or other specialized areas. If the specialized cooking or entertaining will usually be done by someone who is not the primary cook, plan these centers far enough away from the work triangle to keep the cooks from getting in each other's way. A second sink makes a fine addition to an entertainment area.

Checking traffic patterns

After you've planned the activity centers, think about the traffic pattern through the kitchen at different times of day and during parties. Trace the work triangle and door openings on a separate sheet of paper, indicating the traffic flow with arrows. If the traffic must intersect the work triangle at any point, it's best to have it cross the path to the refrigerator.

To redirect traffic, try moving a door, angling a peninsula, or adding an island. Also check whether any appliance doors interfere with traffic. Now's the time to make necessary changes on your plan.

Design: Scale plans & elevations

Once you've blocked out your kitchen space into various activity centers, tentatively positioned your appliances, thought about storage possibilities, checked the traffic pattern, and decided on a basic layout, it's time to draw your floor plan to scale. You'll need to mark all the details of the design you've worked out onto a scale model of your kitchen's perimeter.

It's also time to turn your attention to the walls. To do this, you'll want to draw elevations of each wall, indicating the location and dimensions of all the elements in your kitchen.

Drawing your scale floor plan

To draw your floor plan to scale, you'll need to obtain dimensions of all the appliances you plan to use (see "Kitchen showcase," starting on page 37, for a guide to new appliances). Even if you cannot precisely draw all the details, add the dimensions to make sure the total fits into your given space.

Using the architectural symbols shown on page 21, indicate on the plan where plumbing, gas, and electrical lines enter the room and how they'll reach the appliances (usually from under the floor or through a wall). Also mark the approximate locations of light fixtures, light switches, and electrical outlets. According to code, every countertop longer than 12 inches should have a two-plug outlet. If you're adding a new wall, you may be required to install an outlet every 12 feet, or one per wall regardless of the wall's size. New outlets are placed 12 to 18 inches above the floor or 8 inches above a counter.

On your plan, show which switch operates which light source and indicate whether it's a one-way or multiple switch. Plan to add a three-way switch if your kitchen has more than one entrance. Switches are usually placed 44 inches above the floor.

Mapping elevations

Elevation drawings are actually previews of the new arrangement of structural elements, appliances, and storage units. Because this preview is on paper, you can make changes in the lines, shapes, or proportions of various elements (see page 32) to create a more pleasing and efficient design before you spend a penny.

To complete your elevation drawings, you'll need exact dimensions of doors, windows, and appliances. It will also be necessary to work out storage details for each work center and decide on heights of work surfaces, wall ovens, and hoods.

Counter heights. The height of a work surface affects the height of the storage units above and below it, as well as the placement of any wall oven unit. Depending on your elbow height (see page 24 for explanation), a standard 36-inch-high counter may or may not be comfortable for you. If your elbow height is lower than the average 40 inches, you may want your countertops to be 34 inches or lower; if it's higher, consider making your counters higher. Most appliances are manufactured to fit beneath or along a 36-inch-high counter; drop-in ranges or sinks can be positioned at any height.

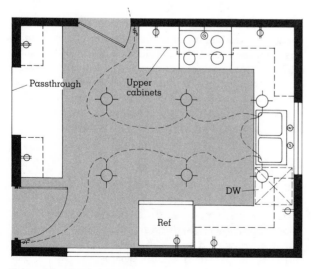

A sample plan
Your final plan drawing should record exact positions and dimensions of all doors, windows, fixtures, and appliances. Use standard architectural symbols to note the approximate locations of plumbing connections and electrical fixtures, outlets, and switches.

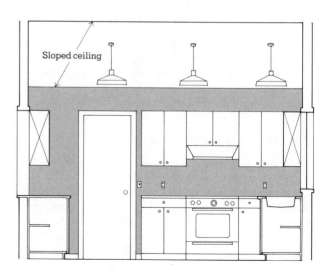

A sample elevation
You'll need to make a drawing for each of your walls, recording exact dimensions of doors, windows, appliances, cabinets, and counters. Elevations should also include dimensions and positioning of a vent hood, hanging light fixture, and other details.

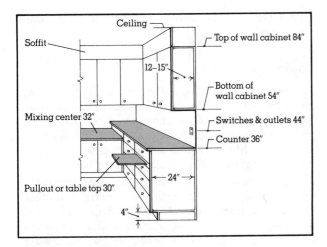

Counter and cabinet heights

Typical heights for counters and cabinets are shown above. Standard base cabinets are 34½ inches high; a countertop adds 1½ inches. The kickspace can be adjusted to raise or lower a cabinet. If you plan two adjacent working surfaces with different heights, the higher counter runs into the corner.

You may want to plan at least one lower or higher work surface if two cooks share a kitchen. A pull-out board, an island of a different height, or a roll-around butcherblock-top cart would solve the problem. When adjacent counters are of different heights, the higher countertop should run into the corner.

To lower the height of prefabricated base cabinets, simply reduce the kickspace at the bottom. Movable wall-mounted units offer greater flexibility in counter and cabinet heights (see page 43).

On separate sheets of graph paper, draw the elevation of each wall, then fill in the counter spaces at the heights most suitable for you.

Storage. To determine the storage needs for each work center, you should sort through all the tools and equipment used at that center. If both base and wall storage is available in an area, decide which items you'd like to place below the work surface and which should go above it. Generally, heavier items are easier to handle at lower levels.

Next, draw a rough sketch of each wall showing the structural elements and appliances. Consider how you'd like the storage on that wall to look and function. Sketch the drawers, cabinets, and pull-out boards you visualize. Do you want open shelves, closed cabinets, or a combination?

When figuring storage for the cooking center, for example, decide whether you'd like your pans on a rack above the cooktop, on a pegboard wall beside the oven, or in a drawer beneath the range. Where should the spices go? Think about all the details and mark the storage locations on your sketch. For more information and ideas on storage, see the photographs on pages 74–79; also see the *Sunset* book *Ideas for Kitchen Storage.*

When you're satisfied with your arrangement, plan the actual dimensions of storage units. Measure tools and equipment, pots and dishes, and any unusually tall or bulky items. Refer to the standard cabinet dimensions and styles shown on page 43. Decide how high and wide a storage unit you'll need to fit your supplies, and which way the door should open. If you're adding drawers, you'll need to determine their height, width, and depth.

Unless you have a dropped ceiling, you'll have space between the top of standard wall cabinets and the ceiling. This space can be enclosed for extra storage, used for light fixtures (soffit lighting, for example), or left open.

Exact measurements are essential for planning cabinets. It's a good idea to have a supplier check your final measurements on the site before ordering the cabinets. If you run into a problem of fit, filler strips—similar to furring strips—can be used alongside a cabinet that butts against a wall. This also compensates for walls that are bumpy or not square. You'll have to use filler strips in the corner if you choose cabinets without face frames showing (full overlay doors, for example). To keep costs down, you might want to buy a few wide cabinets rather than many narrow ones.

While you're working out the storage details, be sure to allow space for future purchases. If you fill every available inch with what you now have, you may soon run into the old problems of clutter and inaccessibility.

When you've determined the exact dimensions of storage units, draw them to scale on the elevation for each wall.

Ventilation. Unless you're planning to buy a range or cooktop with a downventing exhaust system, you'll want to install a hood over the cooking unit. Local codes as well as manufacturers of hoods can give you the required hood width (based on the size of the cooktop) and height from the range. Generally, a hood should extend 3 inches on either side of the cooktop and be placed 21 to 30 inches above it. If you are relocating the range or cooktop, be sure the new location provides an unobstructed route for the hood's exhaust vent pipe. If such route doesn't exist, you'll have to move the range or cooktop, or use a hood that simply filters the air and passes it out again into the room. (This latter type isn't a good first choice, since it won't exhaust moisture and isn't really effective at eliminating odors.)

Other details. Don't forget to include such small details as a hanging light fixture over an eating area, or the height of a backsplash. These and similar items affect your kitchen's design and should be sketched onto the elevation drawings.

Design: Line, shape & scale

The lines, shapes, proportions, and arrangement of storage units and appliances affect the visual space and design of your kitchen. Consider each of these elements as you study your elevation drawings to see how you can best achieve the effect you want.

Looking at lines

Most kitchens incorporate many different types of lines—vertical, horizontal, diagonal, curved, and angular—but often one predominates and characterizes the design. Vertical lines give a sense of height, horizontal lines add width, diagonals suggest movement, and curved and angular lines impart a feeling of grace and dynamism.

Continuity of lines gives a sense of unity to a design. Look at one of your elevation sketches. How do the vertical lines created by the base cabinets, windows, doors, wall cabinets, and appliances fit together? It's not necessary for them to align perfectly. But you should consider such changes as varying the width of a wall cabinet (without sacrificing storage) to line it up with the range or sink. Work out any alterations on a sheet of tracing paper first.

You can follow a similar process to smooth out horizontal lines. Does the top of the window match the top of the wall cabinets? If the window is just a few inches higher, you can either raise the cabinets or add trim and a soffit. If you're including a wall oven, align its bottom with the counter or its top with the bottom of the adjacent wall cabinet.

Depending on the shape and size of your kitchen, you may want to emphasize or minimize a certain line. The long vertical lines created by 42-inch-high wall cabinets (rather than standard 30-inch ones) will make a high ceiling appear even higher. Using a horizontal design on the cabinet fronts or reducing the cabinet height will counteract this effect. A narrow wall benefits from a predominance of horizontal lines; rows of open shelves or tiles on a backsplash visually widen such a wall.

Studying shapes

Continuity and harmony of shapes are also important in achieving a unified design. This doesn't mean exact repetition, which can be monotonous when carried too far. It means, instead, that even when the sizes of objects are different, their shapes can be similar or their arrangement balanced for an overall effect.

Study the shapes created by doorways, windows, cabinets, appliances, peninsulas, islands, and other elements in your kitchen. Are these shapes different, or is there a basic sense of harmony? If you have an arch over a cooking niche, for example, you might want to repeat that shape in a doorway or the trim of an open shelf. Or you could complement an angled peninsula by adding an angled corner cabinet or cooktop unit on the diagonally opposite wall.

Weighing the scale

When the scale of kitchen elements is proportionate to the overall scale of the kitchen, the design appears harmonious. A small kitchen will seem even smaller if fitted with large appliances and expanses of closed cabinets. Open shelves, large windows, and a simple overall design would visually enlarge such a room.

Wall cabinets that extend all the way up to a standard 8-foot-high ceiling can make a room appear top-heavy and small unless the cabinet doors are divided into sections, with smaller doors at the top.

Consider the proportions of adjacent elements as well. Smaller objects arranged in a group help balance a larger item, making it less obtrusive. Check your drawings to see how you can better match the scale of kitchen elements with the scale of the room; the drawing below illustrates this principle.

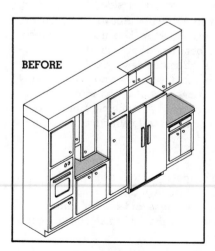

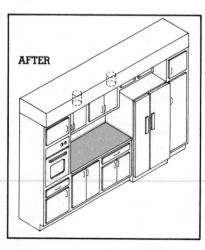

A line change
Too many planes and unmatched lines make the kitchen at far left appear cluttered. Circular knobs seem out of place with the strong vertical look. Refrigerator placement breaks up the counter; the recessed soffit and cabinet over the refrigerator add to the confusion. At left, some simple, inexpensive solutions involve extending the soffit and cabinet over the refrigerator, switching the broom closet and cabinet, cutting off a too-long cabinet, and adding a new countertop and backsplash. Knobs are changed to simple brass pulls. These changes are not only pleasing to the eye, but more efficient as well.

Design: Color, texture & pattern

The choice of colors, textures, and patterns adds impact to your kitchen's design. Colors affect perception of space, control light reflection, and evoke emotional response. Color also emphasizes or camouflages architectural features. As you consider surface colors and textures, it's wise to remember that you have to live with your choices the year around. Bright red or yellow cabinets may add warmth to your kitchen in winter, but they can become overpowering when the summer sun pours in.

Since the quality of light influences the appearance of color, try to select colors under the type of light you'll use in your kitchen (see page 34 for information on kitchen lighting). If you plan to use several colors and textures, make up a pattern board of various materials to judge their compatibility.

Scheming with color

The size and orientation of your kitchen, your personal preferences, and the mood you want to create all affect the selection of your color scheme. Light colors reflect light, making walls recede; thus a small kitchen appears more spacious. Dark colors absorb light and appear to bring objects closer. Use of dark colors can visually lower a ceiling or shorten a narrow room.

When considering colors for a small kitchen, remember that too much contrast has the same effect as a dark color: it reduces the sense of space. Contrasting colors do work well for adding accents or drawing attention to interesting structural elements. If you want to conceal a problem feature, it's best to use one color throughout the area.

Depending on the orientation of your kitchen, you may want to use warm or cool colors to balance the quality of light. While oranges, yellows, or colors with a red tone impart a feeling of warmth, they also contract space. Blues, greens, or colors with a blue tone make an area seem cool—and larger.

A light, monochromatic color scheme (using different shades of one color) is usually restful and serene. Contrasting colors, on the other hand, add vibrancy and excitement to a design. A color scheme with contrasting colors might be too overpowering unless the tones of the colors are varied.

Another possibility when choosing colors would be to include bright, intense colors as accents for furnishings and accessories that can be changed without too much trouble or cost. In any event, your taste, your desire to tie the kitchen area to the rest of the house by using similar colors or textures, or your selection of a favorite wall covering or cabinet style around which to base your color scheme may narrow your choices.

Texture & pattern—for definition

Textures and patterns work like color in defining a room's space and style. The kitchen's surface materials may include many different textures—from shiny tiled backsplash to rough oak cabinets, from matte wallpaper to glossy enameled sink, from quarry tile floor to plastic laminate countertops.

Rough textures absorb light, dull colors, and lend a feeling of informality. Smooth textures reflect light and suggest elegance or modernity. Using similar textures helps unify a design and create a mood.

Pattern choices must also harmonize with the predominant style of the room. Though we usually associate pattern with wall coverings or a cabinet finish, even natural substances such as wood, brick, or stone create patterns. Natural substances generally work well with all textures and colors, even though they add their own qualities.

While variety in textures and patterns adds design interest, too much variety can be overwhelming. It's best to allow a strong feature or dominating pattern to act as the focus of your design, choosing other surfaces to complement rather than compete with it.

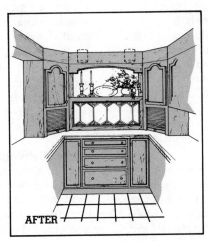

Exchanging clash for class

This kitchen's variety of textures and colors (far left) was overwhelming. The goal: to create an elegant background for the cherry cabinetry, eliminating fluffy curtains, floral wallpaper, butcher-block countertops, and patterned vinyl flooring. The horizontal stained glass window, plate rail, and wooden arch (left) add width to a narrow room. White walls, tile floor, and synthetic marble countertops brighten the area, and allow the cabinets to provide the dominant color accent. Hiding canister lights behind the soffit provides glare-free illumination.

Design: Lighting

No matter how efficient its layout and how interesting its design, a kitchen with poor lighting will be an unpleasant and tiring place to work. A good lighting plan provides shadowless, glarefree illumination for the entire room as well as bright, uniform light for specific tasks. If you plan to dine and entertain in the kitchen, you'll also want to be able to vary the levels of lighting for a softer, more dramatic mood.

When considering your floor plan, you've already thought about how and where to bring in natural light and where to locate light fixtures. These additional details will help you finalize your design.

Natural light

Natural light enters a kitchen through windows or skylights, or both. Though eminently desirable, natural light may illuminate your kitchen unevenly; a single window in the middle of a wall often creates such a strong contrast with the surrounding area that it causes glare. For more even light, consider using two windows on adjacent walls, adding a skylight, or compensating for the glare by illuminating the surrounding area with artificial light.

Depending on your climate and the orientation of windows or skylights, you might need to think of ways to reduce unwanted heat gain or loss or to direct sunlight. The *Sunset* book *Windows & Skylights* offers many suggestions for controlling heat and light.

Artificial light

The selection and placement of artificial light sources require planning. The height of your kitchen ceiling, the decor of the room, and the kind of light sources and fixtures you'd prefer to use are all factors in deciding on a lighting plan.

Incandescent and fluorescent fixtures are the two main sources of artificial home lighting. Either can be used for both general and task lighting, but a combination gives the most pleasing and energy-efficient design.

Several factors may affect your choice of incandescent bulbs or fluorescent tubes: lumens or light output, wattage or the amount of energy used, life expectancy, and price. Though incandescent lighting provides a warmer ambience that's flattering to food and people, it also generates a lot of heat (90 percent of the energy consumed by an incandescent lamp is dissipated as heat) in an already warm environment. Fluorescent lighting operates at a lower temperature and is more energy efficient. Fluorescent tubes also last much longer than incandescent bulbs.

Unlike incandescent lights, a fluorescent tube's lumens and life increase with length and wattage; the longer the tube, the more economical it is to use. When selecting fluorescent lighting, also consider the tube's noise rating (tubes with A rating are the quietest) and whether it starts without delay or flicker.

If you plan to mix incandescent and fluorescent lighting, deluxe warm white (soft white) would probably be the best fluorescent choice; a prime-color lamp that makes all colors equally bright provides the most pleasing light in an all-fluorescent kitchen.

General lighting. General lighting brightens an entire area. There are several ways to provide general illumination for the kitchen. Incandescent fixtures for direct lighting may be recessed, surface mounted, or hanging (pendant lights). Recessed lighting, though unobtrusive, is not very efficient since no light is bounced back into the room from the ceiling or walls. To avoid harsh shadows, place recessed fixtures close enough to each other that their light patterns overlap. To prevent glare, use diffusing shades on pendant and surface-mounted lights.

Fluorescent tubes enclosed in a luminous box mounted on the ceiling spread light down as well as across the ceiling. To illuminate an entire ceiling, place lights behind a valance board between the cabinet tops and ceiling, or illuminate the soffit around the room's perimeter. For softer, indirect lighting, mount incandescent or fluorescent fixtures above the cabinets to wash the ceiling with light.

Whatever type of light source you choose, plan to use dimmers or separate switches to control the level of light. It's easy and inexpensive to put incandescent bulbs on dimmers; the initial cost of dimmers for fluorescents is greater, and the variety of fixtures with dimming devices is limited. To best control fluorescent lighting, place different fixtures on different switches.

Task lighting. Task lighting brings an additional source of light to a specific area. Incandescent fixtures are generally your best choice for task lighting. One of the most popular and inexpensive systems is track lighting. It's particularly well suited for remodeling because it can feed off an existing electrical box and extend around the room's perimeter, lighting several work areas. For best illumination, the track should be installed at least two feet away from a wall (almost the width of a standard counter). To avoid shadows on the work surfaces, point lamps directly over the counters, or place them so that the light comes from the side.

For lighting under cabinets, choose fluorescent tubes or long, narrow, incandescent tubes especially designed for this job (see page 102). To light a cleanup center, position surface-mounted or recessed incandescent fixtures or fluorescent tubes covered with a diffusing panel directly over the sink.

Special lighting. A dimmer switch may achieve the desired light level for dining, but a separate decorative fixture over the eating area helps set it apart from the functional part of the kitchen. If you choose a pendant light, the fixture should be positioned 30 to 36 inches above the table (at least 6 feet above the floor for an eating counter).

ENERGY CONSERVATION IN THE KITCHEN

Because major kitchen appliances account for roughly 15 percent of your home's total energy use, they're a logical target for efforts to save energy—and money. Some of the following suggestions will be useful if you're considering a new appliance; others are reminders for using appliances wisely.

An energy shopping guide

While energy-conserving features on appliances may increase the initial cost, long-term savings usually make the extra investment worthwhile. The Federal Trade Commission's "Energy Guide" labels on appliances estimate operating costs and will help you compare the efficiency of similarly sized models.

The following figures on energy use and savings are averages; your amounts may vary depending upon use, upkeep, and local utility rates.

Refrigerator/freezer. Match the size of a new refrigerator or freezer to your needs. Eight cubic feet of refrigerator space is recommended for two people; add a cubic foot for each additional family member, and 2 extra cubic feet if you entertain frequently. Two cubic feet per person is the suggested figure for a freezer compartment, 6 cubic feet for a separate freezer.

To save up to 16 percent on refrigeration energy costs, look for a power-saver or humid-dry switch that enables you to turn off the anti-sweat heaters (used to remove external condensation) when they're not needed.

Dishwasher. Spray-arm efficiency, rather than water volume, is most important for thorough cleaning. Several consumer publications evaluate the cleaning action of different models.

Some dishwashers are equipped with built-in water heater boosters that raise temperatures to 140°F (60°C). This allows you to set your main water heater between 110° and 120°F (43° to 49°C) and avoid overheating other household water. Automatic air drying lets dishes dry without extra heat, reducing electrical consumption by 30 to 50 percent.

Cooktop, oven & range. Choose a gas range with an electronic ignition instead of pilot lights and you'll lower consumption by as much as 40 percent. Also, an oven door with a window can conserve energy by letting an inquisitive cook view baking progress through a closed door. Each opening of the door wastes 20 to 25 percent of the oven heat.

A microwave oven can use 15 to 70 percent less cooking energy than a conventional oven. Your specific savings will depend on your cooking habits—the types of foods prepared and the frequency of use.

Changing from a conventional oven to a convection oven (a fan circulates hot air around the oven cavity) can save as much as 30 percent of the cooking time and lower the heating temperatures by 25 percent.

Kitchen conservation tips

Besides selecting efficient models, you can also conserve energy by the way you use appliances.

Refrigerator/freezer. Sweating or frost on the unit's exterior can be a symptom of leaking air. Test the doors' gasket seals by closing each door on a dollar bill in several places around the opening. If the dollar pulls out easily, tighten loose door hinges or replace the gasket.

Use a thermometer to set the refrigerator at 38° to 40°F (3° to 4°C) and

open the door as infrequently as possible.

Full freezers stay cold—add bags of ice cubes or milk cartons of water to fill the compartment. Don't add more than will freeze in 24 hours (2 to 3 pounds per cubic foot). In manual defrosting units, keep frost buildup less than ¼-inch thick. Set the temperature at 0°F (−18°C).

Dishwasher. Doing a full load in a dishwasher can use less energy than washing dishes by hand. Rinse plates first with cold water, if needed. Choose a short cycle for lightly soiled dishes and let them air dry (with the door ajar) if you don't have a power-saver option.

Cooktop, oven & range. You can cook several items in the oven at the same time if their cooking temperatures are no more than 50° apart; just set the oven for the average temperature and remove each dish when it's ready.

When boiling foods, use as little water as possible. Covering the pot shortens cooking time and saves 20 percent of the energy.

Conservation & remodeling

You can improve your kitchen's heating, cooling, and lighting by including energy-saving structural improvements during remodeling. Depending on the scope of the project, consider window shading and natural ventilation to prevent overheating, weatherstripping and insulation to stabilize temperatures, and passive solar applications to add warmth and light. For detailed information, see these *Sunset* books: *Do-It-Yourself Energy-Saving Projects, Do-It-Yourself Insulation & Weatherstripping, Windows & Skylights,* and *Solar Remodeling.*

Your final plan

Once you've worked out an efficient layout, planned your storage requirements, and decided on color and lighting schemes, it's time to turn your planning into a final design. But before you draw your revised floor plan, you'll want to consider new appliances, cabinets and countertops, and the myriad choices in floor coverings (see pages 37–44). And you'll need to confront the realities of your budget and your abilities (see pages 45–47).

In considering your total remodeling budget, don't forget such finishing touches as door knobs and drawer pulls, hinges and moldings, curtains and blinds—all the details that pull a design together.

Finalizing your plan

After considering the cost of products, materials, labor, and professional assistance, you may have to adjust your remodeling plans. If your estimated cost exceeds your budget—as is often the case—you'll probably need to reduce costs. Perhaps you can substitute more moderately priced products for your initial choice: would you be willing to settle for less expensive but equally functional lighting fixtures? Or maybe you'll decide to sacrifice one thing in favor of another: would you rather have handpainted tiles and do without a trash compactor?

A substantial difference may signal the need for a substantial reconsideration of your plans. You may have to develop a new and less costly design—often an architect or designer can suggest affordable solutions. You may also want to review your design for any flaws. Recheck your calculations and rethink your priorities. It's far less costly to make changes on paper before you start than it is after work is under way.

Drawing your new floor plan

The planning process culminates with the drawing of your new floor plan (see below). Often called the "working drawing," it is the basis for the remodeling work and for the preparation of a master list of materials. Depending on the extent of your project, you may need one or more building permits before you can start the work. If so, you must submit clear and complete drawings of your existing floor plan and the new one.

Draw the new floor plan the same way you did the existing plan (see page 21). On the new plan, include existing features you want to preserve and all of the changes you're planning to make—new walls, partitions, doors, windows, skylights, light fixtures, electrical outlets, cabinets, countertops, and appliances. If you prefer, you can hire a designer, drafter, or contractor to draw the final plan for you.

For more complicated projects, the building department may require additional or more detailed drawings of structural, plumbing, and wiring changes. You may also need to show areas adjacent to the kitchen on the new plan, so building officials can determine how the project will affect the rest of your house. Elevation sketches are not required, but they'll prove helpful in planning the work and ordering materials.

If you do the ordering of materials for your remodeling project, you should compile a detailed master list. Not only will this launch your work, but it will also keep track of purchases and deliveries. For each item on your list, specify the following information: name and model or serial number, manufacturer, source of material, date of order, expected delivery date, color, size or dimensions, quantity, price (including tax and delivery charge), and a second choice.

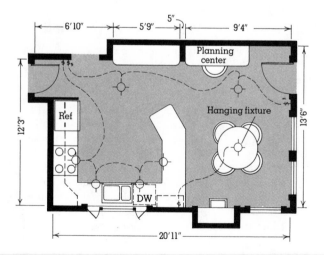

New floor plan

Removing the old partition and counter between the kitchen and breakfast areas and adding an angled peninsula to the opposite side of the room have greatly improved the design.

For the most part, the major appliances remain in their original positions. The refrigerator is shifted a few inches to sit flush with the passage wall, and a 15-inch countertop and base cabinet separate the refrigerator and range, providing necessary set-down space and storage. Wall cabinets are added above the range and refrigerator, and in the corner where the flue used to be.

The windows over the sink are replaced by one larger window. Task lighting comes from downlights over the range, sink, and peninsula, and from under-cabinet lights. Two ceiling-hugging fixtures light the traffic pattern, and a low-hanging fixture over the round table illuminates the eating area. The direction of the back door swing is reversed, and a small planning center is added along the southeast wall.

Another design alternative would be to move the range to the peninsula. Though more costly, this revision would provide additional counter space between the sink and range as well as between the refrigerator and sink.

For a look at the original floor plan and architectural symbols, see page 21.

Kitchen showcase

Choosing appliances and materials can be an exciting—but time-consuming—part of designing and remodeling your kitchen. On these pages we present an illustrated guide to simplify your shopping experience. This mini-showcase offers an overview of styles, functions, installation techniques, and other variables that will form the basis of your selections. The showcase concludes with listings of materials commonly used in the kitchen for countertops and floors.

Tour our showcase before you shop. Though by no means exhaustive, it offers basic information to help you plan your new kitchen.

COOKTOPS

Before confronting the bewildering array of cooking equipment on the market, you'll need to make some decisions. First, which type of energy do you prefer? Gas units heat and cool quickly; the flame is visible and easy to control. Electric units provide low, even heat. Next, think about the style and design. Gas is available with pilot lights or with energy-saving electronic ignition. You can buy a cooktop and one or two ovens as separate units or combined in a single range. One manufacturer offers a cooktop with dishwasher below and conventional radiant oven above—ideal if space is a major consideration. Finishes include stainless steel, enameled cast iron or steel, and brushed chrome. Sizes range from 15 to 47 inches wide, 18 to 25 inches deep, and 3 to 8 inches high (16½ inches high for downventing models).

Style	Characteristics
Conventional  Electric 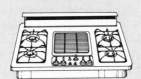 Downventing gas with heavy-duty burner	A conventional gas or electric cooktop is built into a counter like a sink, with connections underneath. Unless you buy a downventing model (more expensive), the unit will require an overhead hood. Downventing cooktops (and ranges) have built-in ventilators that pull out smoke and odors through ducting below. Features include grills, griddles, and rotisseries. Some gas units have three normal burners and one heavy-duty burner that gives off 12,000 BTUs (compared to 8,000 for normal burners).
Convertible  Downventing electric 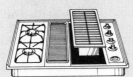 Self-venting gas	Convertible gas or electric cooktops are similar to conventional models, but offer interchangeable and reversible modules that let you replace burners with grill, griddle, and other specialty items.
Smoothtop 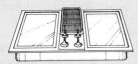 Magnetic induction 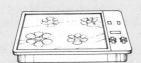 Smoothtop	Electric cooktops with ceramic glass over the coils heat and cool slowly, retaining heat up to an hour after shutoff. They need flatbottom pans for cooking, special products and care for cleaning. Magnetic induction units look like smoothtop but stay cool throughout the cooking process. They operate by creating an electromagnetic field that heats magnetic cookware (cast iron or carbon-core steel). Extremely energy efficient. Quick for small quantities (under 2 quarts); larger volumes cook slowly.
Commercial gas  Commercial 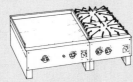 Commercial with griddle	Units are made of heavy-duty cast iron or fabricated metal finished in stainless steel, black enamel, or silver gray. Choice of one to eight burners; many styles combine hot plates or griddles. Need heavy-duty cookware for high burner heat. Simmering is difficult; a cast-iron simmer top is available as an accessory. Usually 6 to 7 inches high with short legs for installing on a base of tile, brick, or other noncombustible material.

WALL OVENS

Built-in ovens save counter space by hiding inside walls. In wall ovens, as with cooktops, you have several choices: conventional gas or electric, microwave, and convection. Double ovens can be installed one above the other, or side by side. Combining a conventional radiant-heat oven with a microwave or energy-saving convection oven is a popular choice. Oven features include built-in warmer shelves, rotisseries, attached meat thermometers, choice of self-cleaning or continuous-cleaning surfaces, variable-speed broilers, and decorator colors or interchangeable door panels.

Style	Characteristics

Radiant

Single with solid door

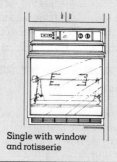

Single with window and rotisserie

Conventional radiant-heat ovens are available in single or double units. Single ovens range from 25 to 32 inches high, 23 to 27 inches wide, and 23 to 28½ inches deep; double ovens may be 44 to 56 inches high, 24 to 27 inches wide, and 23 to 28½ inches deep. Options include continuous or self-cleaning (electric only), door window, removable door, clock and timing device, rotisserie, and automatic temperature probe (oven turns off when food reaches pre-set temperature). One company offers single and double ovens (gas or electric) so well insulated that heat is retained if oven is shut off half to two-thirds of the way into the cooking process.

Microwave

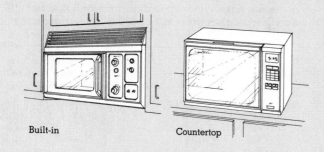

Built-in

Countertop

Foods cook quickly with high-frequency microwaves, but seldom brown. Some models offer a separate browning element; other units combine microwave with radiant or convection cooking. Sizes range from 13 to 17 inches high, 22 to 27 inches wide, and 17 to 22 inches deep. Units can be placed on a counter, built into cabinetry, or purchased as part of a double wall oven or double oven range. Some models, specially designed to be installed above a range (underneath wall cabinets), incorporate a vent and cooking lights; these are wider (30 inches) and shallower (13 to 17 inches deep). Most units open from the right. Features include dial, button, or touch controls, as well as memory bank, programmable cooking, timers, temperature probe, rotisserie, and electronic sensors (automatically calculate cooking time and power levels).

Convection

Convection with meat probe

Microwave and radiant/convection

Gas or electric convection ovens circulate hot air around the oven cavity. More energy-efficient than radiant ovens, they cut cooking time by 30 percent and use reduced temperatures. Good for roasting and baking, less effective for foods cooked in deep or covered dishes (cakes, stews, casseroles). Ovens vary from microwave size to standard range size.

RANGES & HOODS

Ranges combine cooktop and ovens in a single unit; model choices and finishes are as varied as those offered in separate units. Additional features include bottom drawers or broilers and easy-to-clean backsplashes. Take your choice of three types of ranges: freestanding, slide-in (freestanding without side panels to fit between cabinets) and built-in (drop-in). Gas ranges are available with pilot lights or electronic ignition (some states require this energy-saving device on ranges with clocks or timers).

Unless your range is downventing, you'll need a hood over the cooktop. Ducted hoods channel odors, smoke, excess heat, and moisture outside from the kitchen; if exterior venting is impossible, ductless hoods draw out some smoke and grease through charcoal filters. Effectiveness depends on a hood's holding capacity, power of the fan or blower (blowers are quieter and more efficient), and the routing of the ductwork.

Style	Characteristics

Freestanding

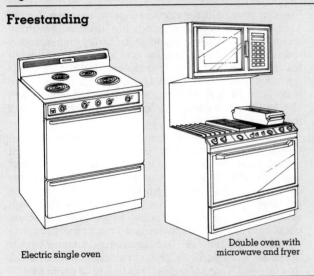

Electric single oven

Double oven with microwave and fryer

Self-contained range rests on the floor, with burners above the oven; some slide in between cabinets. A few units offer an additional upper microwave oven with a built-in ventilator or downventing cooktop. Electric ranges may have coil or smooth cooktops and radiant or convection/radiant ovens. Gas ranges have either radiant or convection ovens; lower ovens may be self-cleaning. Ranges with interchangeable modules offer a deep-fryer accessory. Normal range widths are 30 inches; some 24 or 36-inch models are manufactured. Cooktops on double-oven models may be lower than standard counter height.

Commercial gas ranges may have four to twelve burners, one or two continuous-cleaning, radiant and/or convection ovens, and sometimes a high shelf or broiler at the top. They're not as well insulated as residential units, and they require special care in installation and cleaning. Sizes range from 22 to 70 inches wide, 33 inches deep, and 52½ to 58½ inches high.

Built-in

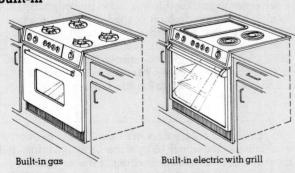

Built-in gas

Built-in electric with grill

Built-in or drop-in ranges have a cooktop with oven below. Permanently installed in specially designed kitchen cabinets (see page 43), the counter-height units rest on a wood base. Models are generally 30 inches wide. Built-in ranges are particularly useful for peninsula or island installation. Though these units have no bottom drawer, the broiler is raised to a convenient height. Gas or electric built-ins offer a choice of finishes, interchangeable cooktop modules, and standard oven accessories.

Hoods

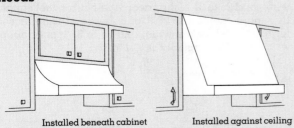

Installed beneath cabinet

Installed against ceiling

A hood should cover the entire cooking area and extend 3 to 6 inches on each side; its bottom edge should be 21 to 30 inches above the cooking surface. The power of a fan or blower is rated in cubic feet per minute (CFM), the loudness in sones; quality hoods handle a minimum of 300 CFM, with a noise level less than 8 sones. Powerful units with variable-speed controls perform quietly; units with ventilators or blowers installed on the roof or exterior wall are most quiet.

REFRIGERATORS & FREEZERS

For efficiency's sake, base your selection of a refrigerator, refrigerator/freezer, or freezer on the size of your family, your shopping habits, and your lifestyle (see page 35 for cubic-foot guidelines). Most refrigerators measure from 27 to 32 inches deep—so they stand out from standard 24-inch-deep base cabinets; only one manufacturer offers relatively expensive 24-inch "built-in" refrigerators (one side-by-side model measures 48 inches wide and has a 30.5 cubic-foot capacity). Finishes include standard appliance colors (enameled or textured), brushed chrome, wood grain, and black glass; some models offer interchangeable door panels.

Consider these features: number and adjustability of shelves, humidity drawers, meat storage compartments, location and range of temperature controls, icemaker and defrost options, direction of door opening, and energy-saving devices such as a power-saver switch. Some models use heat generated by the condenser to eliminate excess moisture, further cutting operating costs.

Style	Characteristics

Refrigerators

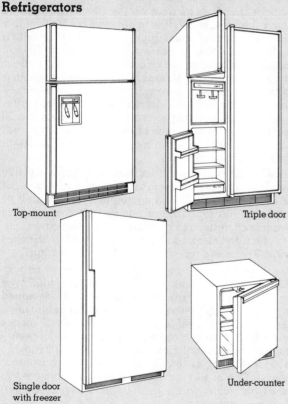

Top-mount

Triple door

Single door with freezer

Under-counter

Popular two or three-door refrigerators permit easy visibility and access to food, but relatively narrow shelves make it difficult to store bulky items. Many side-by-side models offer ice and water dispensers in the door; one model has four shelves in the main door for easy access to frequently used items. Sizes range from 64½ to 69 inches high, 30½ to 36 inches wide, and 28½ to 35 inches deep, with an overall capacity of 18.7 to 27.6 cubic feet.

Double-door refrigerators have the freezer positioned at the unit's bottom or top. The bottom-mount makes it easier to reach the more frequently used refrigerator section; the popular top-mount provides easy storage for large or bulky items, and offers the greatest number of choices in size and design. Top-mount sizes are 56 to 58 inches high, 28 to 33 inches wide, and 27 to 32 inches deep, with an overall capacity of 12 to 32 cubic feet. Bottom-mount units are higher (66 to 68 inches), 28 to 32 inches wide, and 29 to 32 inches deep. Overall capacity is 16.2 to 22 cubic feet.

Though single-door refrigerators are smaller and more economical, their lower cubic-foot capacity (10.6 to 13.9) limits the amount of food that can be stored. Most units must be defrosted manually. Sizes range from 56 to 57½ inches high, 24 to 28 inches wide, and 27 to 29½ inches deep. Under-counter refrigerators are 33 to 34 inches high, 18 to 57 inches wide, and 25 to 32 inches deep, with a 2.5 to 6 cubic-foot capacity.

Freezers

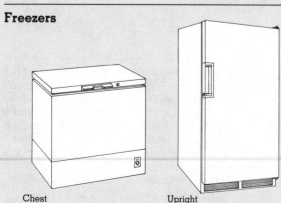

Chest

Upright

Top-opening chest freezers are usually less expensive and more economical to operate than uprights, but most require manual defrosting. Freezer options include power lights, food organizers, and door locks. Chest freezers are 34 to 37 inches high, 25 to 71 inches wide, and 23 to 31 inches deep; their cubic-foot capacity ranges from 5.1 to 28. Uprights are 51 to 70 inches high, 24 to 33 inches wide, and 25 to 32 inches deep, with cubic-foot capacity of 10.1 to 31.1.

SINKS & ACCESSORIES

Commercially available sinks have one, two, or three bowls with or without attached drainboards. Most have predrilled holes for faucets, sprayers, soap or hot water dispensers, or air gaps. Faucet options include a practical washerless, single-lever model. Self-rimming sinks with molded overlaps are supported by the edge of the countertop cutout; flush deck-mounted sinks have surrounding metal strips to hold the basin to the countertop; unrimmed sinks are recessed under the countertop opening and held in place by metal clips. A few integral-bowl sinks are also available.

Material choices include stainless steel (18 or 20 gauge with matte or mirror finish), enameled cast iron, enameled steel or porcelain on steel, as well as brass and copper. Matte-finish 18-gauge stainless steel is the most durable and easiest to keep clean. Stainless steel is relatively noisy; look for a sink with undercoating, or apply your own. Enameled cast-iron sinks have a heavier layer of baked-on enamel than enameled steel, making them quieter and less likely to chip. Elegant, expensive brass or copper finishes require zealous maintenance.

Style	Characteristics

Single bowl

Self-rimming   Flush-mount

Self-rimming with disposer   Bar sink

Single-bowl sinks range from 12 to 33 inches long by 15 to 22 inches wide. Smaller models are large enough for soaking pans, yet don't waste counter space. Some have a small, elevated disposer compartment. Small bar or hospitality sinks come with either a 2 or 3½-inch drain opening; if you're planning to add a disposer, you'll want the larger opening.

Multiple bowls

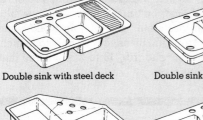

Double sink with steel deck   Double sink

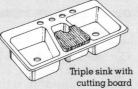

Corner sink   Triple sink with cutting board

Larger than single-bowl units, multiple-bowl sinks measure 33 to 72 inches from side to side, 22 inches from front to back, and offer two or more basins for handling meal preparation and dishwashing simultaneously. In triple-bowl models, the disposer rests in a separate center well. A two-bowl corner sink is a convenient choice for an L-shaped counter. Its overall measurements are 31⅞ inches by 31⅞ inches; each compartment measures 15¾ inches by 4 inches by 7 inches.

Accessories

Hot water dispenser   Disposer

For most sink configurations you can buy cutting boards that fit over the basins to extend counter space, pop-up drains that eliminate the need to fish in the water for sink stoppers, swiveling spouts, and spray-hose attachments. Half-gallon-capacity instant hot water heaters fit underneath sinks; connected to cold or hot water lines, they deliver 190° to 200°F (87° to 93°C) water. Today's garbage disposers handle almost all types of food waste. Look for sturdy motors (½ horsepower or more), noise insulation, and anti-jam mechanisms.

DISHWASHERS

Whether portable or built-in, most dishwashers are standard size: 24 inches wide, 24 inches deep, and 34 inches high. One manufacturer offers a compact 18-inch-wide built-in or portable unit. Standard finishes include enameled steel, brushed stainless, or ¼-inch wood or plastic front panels. Look for such energy-saving devices as a booster heater that raises the water temperature of the dishwasher only, separate cycles for lightly or heavily soiled dishes, and air-drying options. Other features include a delay start that allows you to wash dishes at a pre-set time (during the night instead of at peak-energy hours), prerinse and pot-scrubbing cycles, strainer filtering system, adjustable racks, and rinse-agent dispensers.

Style	Characteristics
Dishwashers Convertible Under-sink	Most built-in dishwashers are installed between base cabinets or at the end of a cabinet. Side panels can be added to the latter to match cabinetry. A space-saving under-sink dishwasher can be installed with a disposer beneath a 6-inch-deep single or double-bowl sink in an area only 24 to 36 inches wide. Portable units come with casters and hoses for attaching to sinks. Some have wood cutting-board tops or a hookup system that allows use of the faucet while the dishwasher is in operation. Most newer models, designed for later conversion to a built-in unit, are front loading.

COMPACTORS

Compactors reduce bulky trash such as cartons, cans, and bottles to a fourth of the original size. A normal compacted load—a week's worth of trash from a family of four—will weigh 20 to 28 pounds. Some models use standard 30-gallon trash bags that can be stored inside the door; others require special bags from the manufacturer; one model can be used without a bag. Look for such features as a toe-operated door latch and key-activated safety switch. Standard appliance colors are available for all models; finish options include black glass with stainless steel, and custom wood panels with or without trim kits. Sizes vary from 12 to 18 inches wide (15 inches is standard), 18 to 24½ inches deep, and 34 to 36 inches high.

Style	Characteristics
Compactors 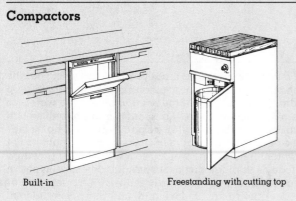 Built-in Freestanding with cutting top	Compactors can be freestanding, built in between cabinets (often near the sink), or added to the end of a counter (similar to a dishwasher). Their height and adjustable kickspace (3 to 4 inches) allow them to blend in with existing cabinetry. Features include reversible manual or automatic doors, separate top-bin door for loading small items (even while the unit is operating), drop-down or tilt-out drawers for easy bag removal, and charcoal-activated filter or deodorizer to control odor. Dimensions and features are exactly the same for freestanding compactors as for built-in models. Freestanding units also offer an optional wooden cutting-block top.

CABINETS

Cabinets determine a kitchen's "personality"; the wide range of available styles and sizes allows you great freedom to create your choice of decor. Whether you select sleek plastic or warm wood, though, careful attention to construction and materials should be your first consideration. There are three basic types of cabinets: base, wall, and special use. Wood finishes range from inexpensive particleboard with wood grain or veneer, to softwoods laminated with hardwood veneers, to expensive hardwood. Plastic and metal cabinets in a variety of colors and textures are also faced with laminated wood. Check on such construction details as interior finish, joints, drawer glides, adjustable shelves, hinges, magnetic catches, and sturdy pulls.

Style

Characteristics

Base

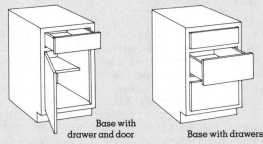

Base with drawer and door

Base with drawers

Base cabinets do double duty, combining storage space with working surface. Though usually equipped with only one top drawer, some base cabinets have three or four drawers, making them particularly useful near sinks and ranges. Standard dimensions are 24 inches deep by 34½ inches high; the addition of a countertop raises them to 36 inches.

Wall

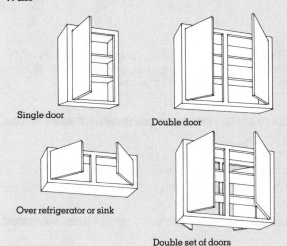

Single door

Double door

Over refrigerator or sink

Double set of doors

Usually mounted on walls, these cabinets can also be hung from the ceiling for peninsula and island installation. Cabinets range from 12 to 15 inches deep and 12 to 33 inches high. The shorter cabinets are typically mounted above refrigerators, ranges, and sinks.

Special use

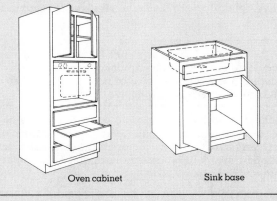

Oven cabinet

Sink base

Manufacturers produce a variety of special-purpose cabinets. You can buy cabinets with cutouts for sinks, built-in ranges, and microwave or slide-in ovens. Before purchasing expensive custom cabinets, look into stock cabinets that can be modified with pull-out boards, turn-around or slide-out shelves, and storage for small appliances.

FLOORING

The vast array of kitchen flooring materials provides a palette that would please an artist. But beyond esthetic considerations, you should weigh the physical characteristics of flooring materials. Will installation involve preparing the subfloor? Can you do the work yourself, or will you need professional assistance? Kitchen floors take a lot of wear and tear: is your choice water-resistant, durable, and easy to clean? Is it hard to walk on or noisy under foot? Many materials are cushioned for comfort and designed to absorb sound.

Type	Characteristics
Wood strip plank wood block	Creates warm decor, resists wear, can be refinished. Water-resistant with polyurethane finish. Needs well-prepared subfloor. Check installation procedure; you may need professional assistance. Moderate to expensive, depending on quality, finish, installation.
Resilient polyurethane sheet vinyl sheet and tile vinyl-asbestos tile rubber tile	Wide range of patterns; some simulate wood, brick, or tile. Flexible, moisture and stain-resistant, easy to install, simple to maintain. Vulnerable to dents and tears, but can be repaired; tiles can collect moisture between seams if improperly installed. Sheets up to 12 feet wide; tiles are 12 inches square. Vinyl and rubber are quiet and comfortable to walk on. Vinyl is least expensive. Polyurethane finish eliminates waxing.
Hard-surface ceramic tile quarry tile slate marble brick	Glazed patterns to unglazed natural colors. Durable; easy upkeep. Hard surface can be cold and noisy. Some are water-resistant; others need seal. Some materials are very heavy—have substructure checked to be sure it can handle the weight. Some ceramic tile is expensive, as is most other masonry flooring.
Carpeting	Sold in rolls or tiles. Durable; industrial carpeting extremely durable. Immediate cleanup is necessary. Absorbs sound, cushions feet. Moderately priced compared to wood, ceramic, and other masonry.

COUNTERTOPS

Forget the plastic or wooden countertops of the past; when new synthetics joined the market, your choices expanded. Today's wood surfaces, generally limited to cutting inserts, can be sealed to prevent staining. Consider marble for baking needs, synthetic marble for complete countertops.

Type	Characteristics
Plastic self-rimmed laminate post-formed laminate vinyl	Wide range of colors and patterns. Plastic resists stains, cleans easily; edges can chip, surface can scorch or burn. Easy installation if measurements are exact. Vinyl is slightly more costly than inexpensive laminate.
Wood butcherblock flooring	Wood, installed by the running foot, is best used as inserts for cutting surfaces. Needs occasional sealing; not heatproof or moistureproof. Polyurethane-coated flooring offers wider choice of natural colors; use only top-grade lumber. Butcherblock is more expensive.
Hard-surface ceramic glass stainless steel tile marble, natural or synthetic	Tile offers widest choice of colors and glazes; some tile needs sealer. Stainless steel tops can be purchased with integral sinks; ceramic glass better used as insert, can't be cut. Expensive marble and synthetic marble need special base support; synthetic is easier to maintain. All hard-surface materials are moderately to very expensive.

Permits, costs & financing

Once you've taken stock of your present kitchen, drawn floor plans and elevations of desired changes, and checked the dazzling array of available fixtures, appliances, and other kitchen materials, you're ready to turn your design into a reality.

This is the time to decide how much of the job you're going to do yourself and to learn how to deal with architects, designers, and contractors (see pages 46–47). It's also the time to determine what local restrictions apply to your proposed remodeling, how much the total job will cost, and how you're going to pay for the project.

Building permits

To discover which building codes may affect your remodeling project and whether or not a building permit is required, check with your city or county building official.

You probably will not need a building permit for simple jobs such as replacing a window with one of the same size, installing a garbage disposer, or changing floor or wall coverings. But for more substantial changes you may need to apply for one or more permits: structural, plumbing, mechanical heating or cooling, reroofing, or electrical.

Before you obtain permits, a building department official—a plan checker or building inspector—may need to see drawings to ensure that your remodeling concept conforms to local zoning ordinances and building codes. If the project is simple, written specifications or sketches may suffice. More complicated projects sometimes require that the design and the working drawings be executed by an architect, designer, or state-licensed contractor.

If you plan to do all the work yourself, you may have to sign an owner-builder release exempting you from workers' compensation insurance (see page 47) before receiving the permits. You don't need workers' compensation insurance if a state-licensed contractor retained by you applies for the permits and does the work.

If you apply for the permits but plan to hire other people to help with the work, you must show a Certificate of Compensation Insurance (see "Hiring workers," page 47).

For your permit you'll be charged a flat fee or a percentage of the estimated cost of materials and labor. You may also need to pay a fee to have someone check the plans.

If you're acting as your own contractor, you must ask the building department to inspect the work as it progresses. A professional contractor handles these inspections without your becoming involved. The number of inspections required depends on the complexity of the remodeling. Failure to obtain a permit or an inspection may result in your having to dismantle completed work.

Figuring costs

Start by making a realistic budget that covers all the supplies you'll need and the cost of any professional help you plan to employ.

Large items, such as appliances, cabinets, and flooring, are easy to remember when computing costs. It's harder to keep track of little items such as nails, glue, and wall switches, all of which can add a tidy sum to your bill. To estimate costs for products and materials, list the tasks you plan to accomplish and the tools, supplies, products, and materials required for each task. Be as detailed as possible.

After your material list is completed, call stores, dealers, manufacturers, and suppliers to obtain prices. Do some comparison shopping. When checking on prices, find out if the items are in good supply or how long you'll have to wait for delivery.

If you're considering working with a professional, wait to complete your material cost estimate until he or she has been hired. Professionals usually have access to a larger variety of products which they can buy at lower prices, and they supply their own tools. If you order your supplies through a professional, your contract should stipulate that he or she is responsible for the condition of the goods, their correctness, and their proper functioning after installation.

Cost of materials is only half the expense of remodeling; the other half depends on who does the job. The more work you do yourself, the more you can cut costs. In addition to honestly evaluating your skills, though, think also of the time required to accomplish each task.

After you have calculated the costs of supplies and professional assistance, compare these costs to your budget. If the total cost turns out to be much higher, you can change your plans to fit the budget. You might also consider remodeling in stages.

Shopping for money

If you're like most homeowners, you'll finance your remodeling project by arranging some kind of loan. Before making any loan arrangements, though, you must have finished plans and specifications for your project and accurate cost estimates of materials. If you plan to do the work yourself, be sure your material costs are complete; if you're using professionals, they will supply this information.

It's important to shop as carefully for financing as you do for any of your new kitchen supplies. Some of the sources you might borrow against for remodeling money are life insurance, retirement or profit-sharing funds, savings accounts, or stocks and bonds. Your home is one of your biggest assets—consider refinancing, or look into a second mortgage. Because lending laws vary from state to state, check the details of these methods as they apply to your situation.

Working with professionals

Major home remodeling projects are not easy work. Some you can do yourself; others may require some professional help. Still others may be best left completely in the hands of professionals.

What jobs require professional help? How can you get the help you need? What is the best way to work with professionals? If you're confronted with questions like these, you'll find the following suggestions helpful as you plan and carry out your remodeling project.

When do you need professional assistance?

The effort you can contribute to any project depends on your knowledge, your abilities, your patience, and your stamina. If you know how to draw plans but dislike physical labor, you'll need someone else to perform the actual work. If you're able to wield a saw and hammer but can't draw a straight line, you may need professional help only to prepare working drawings.

Some people prefer to do the nonspecialized work, such as clearing the site for construction and cleaning up later, but hire experts for everything else. Others let professionals handle all the tasks from drawing plans through applying the finishing touches.

No matter whom you consult, be as precise as possible about what you want. Collect pertinent photographs from magazines, manufacturers' brochures, and advertisements. Describe the materials, appliances, fixtures, and fittings you want to use. Provide working plans and some idea of your budget. If you have questions, write them down before the interview. The more information you can supply, the better job a professional will be able to do.

Remember, too, that your home is an expression of your family's identity. Whether you're adding rooms or remodeling existing space, it's more than just a construction project; it's a personal project. In choosing a professional, you'll want to find someone who is not only technically and artistically skilled but with whom you and your family feel comfortable and compatible.

You don't want to consign your remodeling efforts to a professional who will ignore your ideas and impose his or her own standards. You do want a person who will take your ideas seriously and bring an increased measure of knowledge, skill, judgment, and taste to the project. Admittedly, it's difficult to tell beforehand how well any professional will work with you; if you're concerned with a good working relationship, though, you should direct your attention to that subject as well as to technical ones when you make your choice.

Architect or building designer—which one do you need?

Either an architect or a building designer can draw plans acceptable to building department officials; each can also specify materials for a contractor to order. He or she can send out bids, help you select a contractor, and supervise the contractor's performance to ensure that your plans and time schedule are being followed. Some architects and designers even double as their own contractors.

Most states do not require designers to be licensed, as architects must; designers may charge less for their labor. If stress calculations must be made, designers need state-licensed engineers to design the structure and sign the working drawings; architects can do their own calculations.

Many architects are members of the American Institute of Architects (AIA), and many designers belong to the American Institute of Building Designers (AIBD). If you're working with kitchen or bath designers, look for members of the National Kitchen and Bath Association (NKBA) or the Society of Certified Kitchen Designers (SCKD). Each association has a code of ethics and a continuing program to inform members about the latest building materials and techniques.

Architects and designers may or may not charge for time spent in an exploratory interview. You'll probably be charged for plans on an hourly basis. If you want an architect or designer to select the contractor and keep an eye on construction, plan to pay either an hourly rate or a percentage of the cost of materials and labor—10 to 25 percent is typical. Descriptions of the services and amount of the charges should be stated in advance *in writing* to prevent later expensive misunderstandings.

If your project is very small, you may be able to entice an apprentice or drafter working in an architect's or designer's office to draw plans for you. Plan to pay by the hour.

Choosing a contractor

Contractors do more than construction. Often they're skilled drafters, able to draw plans acceptable to building department officials; they also can obtain the necessary building permits. A contractor's experience and technical know-how may even end up saving you money.

Selection. If you decide to use a contractor, ask architects, designers, and friends for recommendations. To compare bids for the actual construction, contact at least three state-licensed contractors; give each one either an exact description and sketches of the desired remodeling, or plans and specifications prepared by an architect or designer. Include a detailed account of who will be responsible for what work.

Don't be tempted to make price your only criterion for selection; reliability, quality of work, and on-time performance are also important. Ask the contractors for the names and phone numbers of their customers. Call several and ask them how they feel about the contractor; if you can, inspect the contractor's work.

Check bank and credit references to determine the contractor's financial responsibility. Your local Better Business Bureau is also a good source of information about an individual's reputation.

Fees. Most contractors will bid a fixed price for a remodeling job, to be paid in installments based on the amount of work completed. Many states limit the amount of "good faith" money that contractors can request before work begins.

Though some contractors may want a fee based on a percentage of the cost of materials and labor, it's usually wiser to insist on a fixed-price bid. This protects you against both an unexpected rise in the cost of materials (assuming that the contractor does the buying) and against the chance that the work will take more time, adding to your labor costs.

Contract. Make sure your agreement with the contractor you've selected includes the following items in writing: plans and material specifications, services to be supplied, cost, method and schedule of payment, time schedule, and warranty against defects. Not only is the contract binding to both parties, but also it minimizes problems by defining responsibilities. Changing your mind once construction starts usually requires a contract modification, involving both additional expense and delays.

Selecting a kitchen designer

Choosing a kitchen designer is very much like choosing a contractor. Describe your project to several designers and ask to see examples of their work—photographs or plans of recently completed jobs. If possible, call on several of their past customers, checking on the creative approach, workmanship, and detailing of the finished kitchen. Get at least three bids for comparison purposes.

For interior design

Unless you're working with a kitchen designer, you may wish to call on the services of an interior designer for finishing touches. These experts specialize in the decorating and furnishing of rooms. They can offer fresh, innovative ideas and advice. Through their contacts, a homeowner has access to materials and products not available at the retail level. Many designers belong to the American Society of Interior Designers (ASID), a professional organization.

Interior designers work on an individual basis. Their approaches differ, depending on the type and size of the project. A preliminary interview is customary to discover whether you can work effectively with the designer.

Expect to be charged an hourly fee or a percentage of all merchandise purchased for the project.

Hiring subcontractors

When you act as your own general contractor and put various parts of your project out to bid with subcontractors, you must use the same care you'd exercise in hiring a general contractor.

You'll need to check the references, financial resources, and insurance coverage of a number of subcontractors. Once you've received bids and chosen your subcontractors, you should work out a detailed contract for each specific job and carefully supervise all the work.

Though this process will be time-consuming, you'll save money and have much more control over the quality of the work.

Hiring workers

Even when you're operating as your own contractor and hiring subcontractors, you may want to hire workers on an hourly basis for their specialized skills.

Workers' compensation insurance. If you hire such help, you may have to provide workers' compensation insurance to cover possible job-related injuries. Though provisions vary from state to state, compensation insurance usually reimburses the worker for wages lost and for the cost of medical treatment. Workers' compensation policies are available from insurance brokers, insurance companies, and sometimes from state funds.

Taxes. If you employ people directly and if they earn more than a minimum amount set by the state, you must register with the state and federal governments as an employer. You will be required to withhold and remit state and federal income taxes; withhold, remit, and contribute to Social Security; and pay state unemployment insurance.

For information, talk to a building department official, or look under the subheading "Taxes" listed under your state in the telephone directory.

Where to look for assistance

The best way to find competent architects, designers, contractors, and workers is to ask friends and neighbors who used professionals in a project similar to yours. You can also seek referrals from retail building materials outlets (listed in the Yellow Pages under "Hardware" and "Lumber").

The Yellow Pages list design professionals under "Architects," "Building Designers," "Interior Decorators and Designers," "Kitchens," or "Drafting Services"; look for contractors to handle a remodeling project under "Contractors—Alteration" and contractors for major projects under "Contractors—Building, General." The Yellow Pages are also a good source for more specialized assistance.

DESIGN IDEAS

Layouts · Materials · Lighting · Storage

Everyone knows a picture can be worth a thousand words; that's the reason for this chapter. It's packed with full-color photos showing kitchen design ideas you can apply to your own situation, whether you're remodeling or starting from scratch.

The material is organized into sections. The first, "Basic floor plans" (pages 50–53), presents fundamental layouts and their variations. Even though you may not have a choice of floor plan, study the photos in this section carefully: you're likely to find details that apply to any kitchen. A related section, "Family connections" (pages 54–59), deals with the relationship of the kitchen to the rest of the house—always an important consideration.

"On the surface" (pages 60–63) shows good ways to use surfacing materials ranging from plastic laminate to stone. "Bright ideas" (pages 64–67) explores natural and artificial lighting—almost always subject to improvement when you're remodeling, and an important concern if you're designing a new kitchen. Two related sections, "Designs for the cooking couple" (pages 68–69) and "Dividing the work" (pages 70–73), illustrate the idea of separate work centers—a key to real kitchen efficiency. "Planning for storage" (pages 74–79) concludes this chapter.

Attention to details of line, shape, and color in overall design make this compact kitchen look and feel larger. Wood veneer is matched across cabinet faces; tile surfaces harmonize. The four black tiles at left are the "burners" of a magnetic-induction cooktop. Architect: Bert W. Tarayao.

Basic floor plans

Corridor kitchen
Compact kitchen shows how a corridor,
or "pullman," layout concentrates
maximum counter space in minimum
square footage. Work areas are located
along a single counter; the opposite
counter serves as space for overflow and
serving. Placement of a refrigerator
across the corridor from the sink creates
an efficient work triangle. Architect:
Bob Easton Design Associates.

L-shaped kitchen with island

Adding an island to the basic L-shaped plan gives excellent separation of work areas, while maintaining a compact work triangle. The layout provides greatly expanded counter space, with plenty of room for a cook and several helpers. The island also offers an alternate location for a cooktop or sink and helps direct traffic away from the work areas. Design: European Kitchens & Baths.

L-shaped kitchen

Folding the one-counter corridor plan into an L helps concentrate the work triangle while increasing counter space. Traffic flow tends to by-pass the cook. In the kitchen shown, carousel storage shelves are located at the bend in the L, making use of space potentially lost in corner cabinets. Architect: Jay Fulton.

. . . Basic floor plans

Extra counter

Plans called for a high, narrow counter at the rear of an L-plus-island configuration. The raised counter serves as a planning center; shelves beneath house cookbooks. The island food-preparation area contains a sink and baking center. The large mixer rides up on a typewriter lift. Architect: Robert Hubner.

U-shaped kitchen

Floor plans based on a U-shaped layout yield maximum counter space, excellent work triangles, and minimum disruption from family traffic. In this kitchen, the nearest leg of the U serves as an eating bar, or as extra space for ambitious culinary projects. Architect: William B. Remick.

U-shaped kitchen with island

Large kitchen features separate cooking areas on opposite legs of the U; a butcherblock island acts as the preparation center for both, and for the wall ovens located across the traffic corridor. Central sink location facilitates cleanup, whichever cooking area is in use. Design: European Kitchens & Baths.

Family connections

Disappearing trick

Glass-door cabinets, large pass-through and heightened doorway seem to "dissolve" the wall in this kitchen remodeling project, giving it a lively connection to the breakfast room beyond. Design: Agnes Bourne.

Coming of age

Careful remodeling adds modern living concepts to an 1869 house without changing its character. Family room replaces a former maid's room and bath. Kitchen cabinetry evokes the old, but is all new. Glass cabinet doors and generous openings between rooms enhance the now-spacious feeling. Architect: Glen William Jarvis.

Communication gap

New opening keeps cook and family united and visually expands both kitchen and dining room. Basically an extension of the original doorway at right, the enlarged arch also defines a new, informal eating bar in the dining room. Design: Nancy Cowall Cutler.

Country harmony

When a remodeled kitchen is opened up to the family room, planning for a continuity of materials helps tie the rooms together. Here brick, wood-mimicking vinyl flooring, and natural wood finishes combine for a truly unified kitchen and family room. Design: Diane Johnson Design.

. . . Family connections

Heart of the house
Kitchens are often the focus of family activity. This one is nicely linked to the rest of the house by means of an opening to the family room at right, and a pass-through to a new breakfast room to the left. Added backsplash behind the cooktop hides kitchen clutter from view. Design: European Kitchens & Baths.

Seeing eye to eye
Raised eating and lounging area invites eye-level communication with the cook, for both family meals and entertaining. When visual separation is desired, a miniblind drops from a concealed pocket just above the bilevel counter dividing kitchen and lounge. Architect: Michael D. Moyer.

Effective countermeasures

View from the family room shows how an
extra-deep counter serves two areas at
once. There's space for shelves and
television on the family room side, with
plenty of depth left over on the kitchen
side for full-size cabinets. Rollaway doors
hide the TV when it's not in use.
Architect: William B. Remick.

... **Family connections**

Islands in the stream

It's easy to imagine the convivial ebb and flow that takes place around these modern, tomato-red kitchen islands set so frankly in the midst of an outsized yet gracious old living room. Designed with entertaining in mind, the arrangement provides plenty of space for several cooks and helpers. Two sinks, each with dishwasher, speed things along. And there's always a seat by the fire for those not involved in preparing the meal. Architect: Brett Donham. Kitchen designer: Katherine Warden.

Contemporary continuity

In this new home, the kitchen occupies one end of a large family room. Traffic flows between kitchen and planning center at right; an eating bar hides the cooking area from view. Refrigerator, ovens, pantry, and closet are built into a blocklike projection of the back wall. A wooden soffit circles the entire room, tying everything together. Design: Shirley Freeborn.

Low profile

This small house is essentially a single large room with counters acting as the only barriers in the social spaces. Low freezer and refrigerator made it possible to build most of the kitchen into a single counter unit; dining and living areas lie beyond. Architects: Buff and Hensman.

On the surface

Tile on tile
Hand-painted tile backsplash and plain tile countertop make a pleasing combination in this friendly kitchen. A practical wooden edge matches the cabinetry; unlike tile, it's easy to repair if nicked or chipped. Design: Nancy Cowall Cutler. Tile design: De Muth Handpainted Tile.

High-tech spoken here
Stainless steel island, refrigerator, and range shine softly against a background of white plastic laminate cabinets and white tile floor. Reflective surfaces and excellent ambient and task lighting ensure that this kitchen is always ready for serious cooking.

Enduring stone

Nearly indestructible, stone is one of the most handsome—and most costly—materials used for kitchen surfaces. Here, polished granite countertops and a flagstone floor harmonize in a composition of understated elegance. Architect: MLA/Architects. Interior designer: Stephen Chase.

Old craft meets modern technology

Full-height backsplash of large geometric tiles is complemented by space-age synthetic marble countertops; resin inlay strips match the tile's blue trim. Design: Olivieri Quinn Associates.

... On the surface

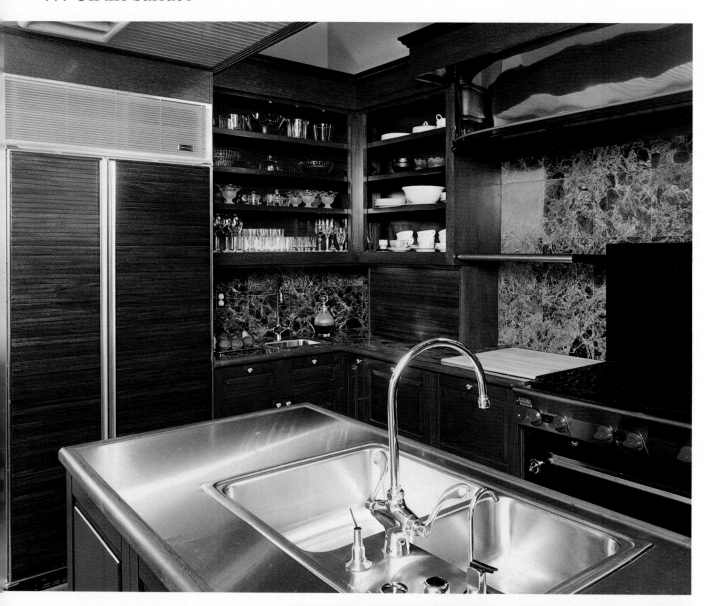

Colorful orchestration

Complex harmonies of stainless steel, mahogany, marble, and brass distinguish an older home's kitchen. The wooden counter edge saves the expense of a fabricated steel edge on the near counter, a stone edge on the far counter. Marble tiles are a simple way to introduce the practical luxury of stone into the kitchen composition. A chopping block next to the stove covers a grill unit beneath. Design: Osburn Design.

An appropriate combination

You really shouldn't cut on tile, but it's great for hot pots and wet sinks; wood's best for cutting, but it's not happy around water, and hot pots can burn it. This solution—a tile countertop with generous butcherblock inserts—uses both materials to best advantage. Architect: Glen William Jarvis.

Keeping it simple
Crisp, modern design combines laminate counters and lower cabinets with upper cabinets of glass and painted wood. Tile pads set into the counters near the cooktop and ovens serve as "landing pads" for hot pots. An oak accent strip on the counter edges buffers the brittle laminate against impacts. Architect: Steven Goldstein.

Fresh look at traditional materials
Sleek kitchen achieves a futuristic effect with traditional materials: butcherblock in the food-preparation area, tile in cooking and cleanup areas (even the magnetic-induction cooktop uses tiles over heating elements). A copper-faced hood complements the warm oak cabinets and floor. Architect: Marshall Lewis.

Bright ideas

Opening up for light and air

Enlarged kitchen-breakfast area pushes out into a new greenhouse extension, gaining lots of natural light in the process. Large windows slide open on warm days, turning the room into a delightful open-air gallery. Design: European Kitchens & Baths.

Light from above

Tucked away in a nearly windowless location, this kitchen was once a dark cave. Now it sees the light through a 3 by 18-foot skylight. Recessed fixtures add light at night and on cloudy days; three track lights focus extra light on food-preparation areas. Existing structural members of the house's flat roof pass unobstructed through the shallow skylight shaft. Architect: William B. Remick.

Razzle-dazzle

Virtuoso display of exposed framing, high clerestory windows, and gallons of white paint are the keys to this kitchen daylighting design. When the sun isn't on the job, high-intensity quartz lights keep work areas bright. Architect: Richard Sygar.

. . . Bright ideas

A touch of tradition

Small lamps shed gentle, even illumination on this sink counter and pass-through, harmonizing with other lamps in the rest of the house. Two can lights, nearly concealed within the overhanging pot rack, provide much stronger light when needed. Architect: Weston Whitfield.

Light where it's needed

When a kitchen is open to the roof line, it's often difficult to light central areas. Here, a sleek modern office fixture drops low to evenly illuminate a bilevel counter, benefiting cooks and guests alike. Design: Marilyn Woods and Brian Grossi.

Simplicity is the key

This large skylight opening brings in plenty of daylight, yet there are only two (much smaller) skylights on the roof. The design provides much of the even light distribution of a very large skylight, while saving expense. Ceiling joists were left in place, clad in fir—a further saving. Architect: Robert Peterson.

Designs for the cooking couple

Out of the ordinary

Closing off a pass-through was the key to converting a conventional kitchen to one designed for a cooking couple. Above, ovens and refrigerator are located in the former pass-through area, freeing space for a second cooking station, right. The new design also includes a pastry center with generous appliance garages, and a butcherblock surface set below counter level for easy bread kneading. Design: Nancy Cowall Cutler.

Gourmet treat

New kitchen for a pair of expert cooks shows just how far you can go when you're really committed. The kitchen takes up space formerly occupied by an old kitchen, small bedroom and bathroom, laundry, butler's pantry, service porch, and hallway. At left, a built-in charcoal broiler and gas-fired wok are located on one side of the island, with a pastry slab in the foreground; desk, bar sink, microwave, refrigerator, and wall ovens are in the background. Below, separate cook stations with three commercial burners apiece take up most of the island's other side. Exposed brick flue serves a furnace in the basement. Countertops of synthetic marble, stainless steel, and granite are used where most appropriate. The straightforward cabinets feature extensive drawer storage for efficient access. Design: Carlene Anderson.

Dividing the work

One for cooking, one for cleanup

Even in a small kitchen, two sinks are better than one. The sink in the foreground is part of a food-preparation island; it's equipped with a garbage disposer and instant hot water dispenser. The sink in the background occupies one end of a cleanup center, with a dishwasher below. (For another view, see photo, page 54.) Countertop materials vary according to purpose: synthetic marble in the cleanup area, where it's likely to be wet; butcherblock on the island, for chopping and kneading. Design: Agnes Bourne.

A step further

Two views of the same kitchen show a plan organized around a pair of work centers: one for cooking (below), and one for cleanup (left). Traffic flows between the two centers at the point from which the photographs were taken. Countertop materials depend on use: impervious tile in the potentially wet cleanup area, butcherblock in the cooking area. Both centers incorporate extensive storage in modular cabinets. Design: European Kitchens & Baths.

. . . Dividing the work

Stowaway

Compact baking center comes out of hiding, rolls to any part of the kitchen, then tucks away neatly in a counter end when work is done. The marble top is great for pastry and candy making; tilt-out bins below store flour and sugar. Baking gear is stored in the lowest compartment. Architect: William B. Remick.

Supercenter

Mild-mannered cabinets (above) conceal super powers of storage and organization (right). Built for a serious pastry cook, this baking center features everything needed in one well-thought-out unit. The granite top is both pastry slab and landing place for hot dishes; beneath it, a bread board and a pair of ovens coexist with a wealth of storage that leaves no space untapped. Design: Carlene Anderson.

Multipurpose buffet

Kitchen buffet counter drops down at one end to become a desk and computer center. A small electric typewriter stores in the drawer at left; the drawer fronts below hide a single large drawer that stores suspended files. Design: Marilyn Woods and Brian Grossi.

Logical extension

Planning center occupies one end of a large island that also contains a cooktop, eating bar, and food-preparation center with a small sink. In a pinch, the planning center can double as a kitchen work surface, since it's simply an extension of the butcherblock island. Architect: Fisher-Friedman Associates.

Planning for storage

Making the most of available space
Semicircular swing-out shelves reclaim space that might be lost in a "blind" corner. Once swung open, these shelves pull out of the cabinet for complete access to their contents. The overall kitchen design features large storage drawers, laminate surfaces, and a granite pastry slab inset in the counter. Architect: Bob Easton Design Associates.

Touring a designer's kitchen

Drawer beneath the cooktop, *below left*, holds pots at the ready; lids rest in a divided drawer below. The spice drawer allows easy access to tilted jars. *Below right*, roll-out shelves disclose a trash can and cleaning supplies; tilting trays reclaim space usually lost between the sink and cabinet face. Carousel trays, *bottom left*, provide convenient access to corner storage. Banks of drawers prove more efficient than regular cabinets with shelves. Two drawers are sized to standard box dimensions. The eating bar, *bottom right*, features slide-out shelves perfect for cereal and snack boxes; it is located out of the kitchen mainstream so family members can help themselves. In the background, ovens and an appliance garage are set into the wall to save space. Design: Carlene Anderson.

. . . Planning for storage

When space is deep and narrow

Pull-out rack turns a deep, narrow niche beside the refrigerator into effective, accessible storage space. The unit is part of a modular European cabinet system; similar pantries can be built using widely available hardware. Architect: Steven Goldstein.

Designing for what you'll store

Modular European cabinets illustrate an adaptable idea: plan the cabinet for what you'll put in it. At left, wire baskets slide out, revealing their entire contents at a glance; a similar space at right houses fixed shelves for large bowls and cooking gear. Drawers below are easy to reach without crouching or stooping. Design: European Kitchens & Baths.

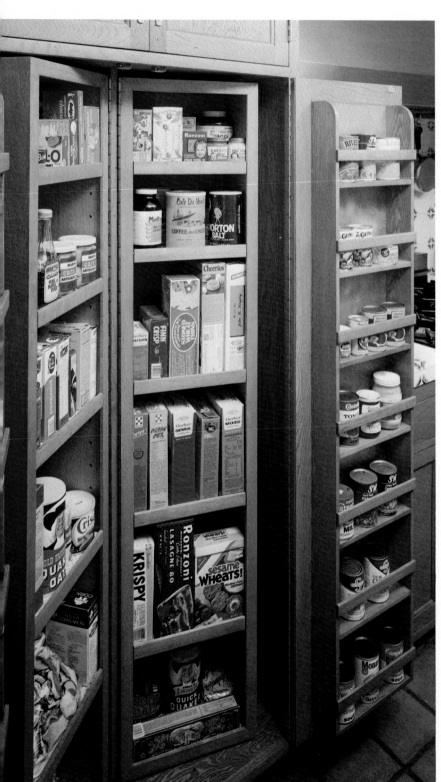

Maximum storage in a standard cabinet

This pantry makes maximum use of standard cabinet dimensions. Door-mounted shelves, two-sided fold-out shelves, and more shelves at the back of the cabinet ensure easy access to every bit of space. Capacity is large, yet nothing gets lost. Design: Sarah Lee Roberts.

When space is shallow and wide

This pantry divides available shelf depth between the doors and the cabinet. Most goods are displayed in single ranks for simple selection and inventory. Architect: Hiro Morimoto/Atelier Architects.

... Planning for storage

Time traveler
This fine old veteran got a new lease on
life when refinished and fitted with
modern refrigeration equipment. Now
it's an eminently practical refrigerator of
large capacity and marvelous looks. An
added touch: the compressor was
mounted below floor level, to isolate noise.
Architect: Glen William Jarvis.

Never give away an inch

Appliance garages have become
standard items in kitchen remodeling
schemes, but they can cost valuable
counter space. To save that space, this
pair of garages was set into and through
the wall; much of their depth lies outside
the house (the small green shed seen
through the window is the roof of the
garage). Design: Carlene Anderson.

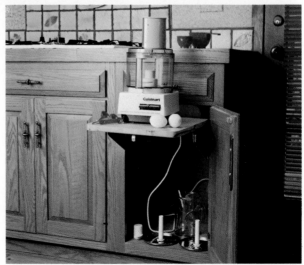

Rising to the occasion

Spring-up shelves, or typewriter lifts,
work as storage shelves when down, as
work surfaces when up. They're just the
thing for food processors and heavy
mixers, and can be adapted to most
cabinets. Design. Rick Sambol.

Professionally designed and owner-built, this renewed kitchen amply repays the effort. The design combines a raised ceiling, new skylight and bay window, a clean and functional layout, and all-new cabinetry and floor. Design: Rick Sambol.

REMODELING BASICS

Installation · Removal · Tools · Techniques

Remodeling a kitchen means different things to different people. A minor task, such as adding a row of track lights to illuminate a dark area or brightening your walls with new coverings, can transform the whole space and satisfy you with the fresh new look. Perhaps, though, you're ready to begin a major overhaul—relocate the sink, install a dishwasher and garbage disposer, move a wall, lay a tile floor, or open the ceiling with a skylight.

This chapter touches on all aspects of kitchen remodeling; you'll find information on dismantling as well as installing everything from appliances to windows. If you're planning only a few improvements, turn directly to the sections in which you're interested. Instructions for replacing wall cabinets or countertops, for example, can be found under "Cabinets & countertops" on pages 108–113. Do you need new wall coverings to complement those cabinets? Turn to the section on "Walls & ceilings," pages 103–107.

Can you do the job yourself? Our directions assume that you have some knowledge of basic tools, building terms, and techniques—how to hammer a nail, use a straightedge, and handle an adjustable wrench. If you need more detailed information on step-by-step procedures, take a look at the *Sunset* books *Basic Carpentry Illustrated*, *Basic Plumbing Illustrated*, and *Basic Home Wiring Illustrated*.

Before work begins

Are you ready to remodel? Before plunging into a project, you should form a clear idea of the sequence of steps necessary to complete the job, obtain any necessary permits from your local building department, and evaluate your own ability to perform each of the tasks. To do the work yourself, you'll also need to provide yourself with the proper materials and tools.

After you have a clear understanding of what's involved, you're ready to begin.

Can I do the work myself?

The level of skill required to remodel your kitchen depends on the scale of the improvements. Surface treatments—such as painting, wallpapering, replacing light fixtures, hanging cabinets, or laying resilient flooring—are within the realm of any homeowner with the rudiments of do-it-yourself ability. Some projects may require a few specialized tools, generally available from a building supply or home improvement center.

If you're still hesitant about your talents, register for some of the "how-to" classes often available through adult education programs. In such classes you'll learn basic techniques and acquire practical experience without making a costly mistake on your home.

Complex remodeling tasks—such as moving bearing walls, running new drain and vent pipes, or wiring new electrical circuits and service panels—are often best handled by professionals. Many smaller jobs within the structural, plumbing, and electrical areas, though, are within the skills of a homeowner with basic experience.

Planning your attack

As the scale of your remodeling project increases, the need for careful planning becomes more critical. Before the work begins, double-check the priorities listed below.

- Establish the sequence of jobs to be performed, and estimate the time required to complete each one.

- If you're getting professional assistance, make sure you have firm contracts and schedules with contractors, subcontractors, or other hired workers.

- Obtain all required building permits (see page 45).

- Arrange for delivery of materials; be sure you have all the necessary tools on hand.

- If electricity, gas, or water must be shut off by the utility company, arrange for it before work is scheduled to begin.

- Find out where you can dispose of refuse, and secure any necessary dumping permits.

- Be sure there is a storage area available for temporarily relocating fixtures or appliances.

- Measure fixtures and appliances for clearance through doorways and up and down staircases.

Your goal is to maintain an operating kitchen during as much of the time as possible. With careful scheduling and planning, the remodeling siege can be relatively comfortable for the entire family.

How to use this chapter

The sections in this chapter are arranged in the order in which you'd proceed if you were installing an entirely new kitchen. Read consecutively, they'll give you an overview of the scope and sequence of kitchen improvements.

The first three sections survey the relatively complex subjects of structural, plumbing, and electrical systems. Whether or not you plan to do the work yourself, you'd be wise to review these sections for background information. A knowledge of your home's inner workings enables you to plan changes more effectively and to understand the reasons for seemingly arbitrary code restrictions affecting your plans.

Some of your most difficult re-modeling hours may be spent tearing out old work. To minimize the effort, we've included removal procedures within the appropriate installation sections.

If you're planning only one or two simple projects, turn directly to the applicable sections for step-by-step instructions. Special features within the chapter present additional ideas and information for maximum improvement with minimum work and expense.

STEPS IN REMODELING

You can use this chart to plan the basic sequence of tasks involved in dismantling your old kitchen and installing the new one. Depending on the scale of your job and the specific materials you select, you may need to alter the suggested order. Manufacturers' instructions offer additional guidelines.

Removal sequence

1) Accessories, decorative elements
2) Furniture
3) Contents of cabinets, closets, shelves
4) Fixtures, appliances
5) Countertops, backsplashes
6) Base cabinets, wall cabinets, shelves
7) Floor materials
8) Light fixtures
9) Wall coverings

Installation sequence

1) Structural changes: walls, doors, windows, skylights
2) Rough plumbing changes
3) Electrical wiring
4) Wall and ceiling coverings
5) Light fixtures
6) Wall cabinets, base cabinets, kitchen islands, shelves
7) Countertops, backsplashes
8) Floor materials
9) Fixtures, appliances
10) Furniture
11) Decorative elements

Structural basics

Acquiring a basic understanding of your kitchen's structural shell is required homework for many kitchen improvements. Your kitchen's framework probably will conform to the pattern of the "typical kitchen," shown in the illustration below.

Starting at the base of the drawing, you'll notice the following framing members: a wooden sill resting on a foundation wall; a series of horizontal, evenly spaced floor joists; and a subfloor (usually plywood sheets) laid atop the joists. This platform supports the first-floor walls, both interior and exterior. The walls are formed by vertical, evenly spaced studs that run between a horizontal sole plate and parallel top plate. The primary wall coverings are fastened directly to the studs.

Depending upon the design of the house, one of several types of construction may be used above the kitchen walls. If there's a second story, a layer of ceiling joists rests on the walls; these joists support both the floor above and the kitchen ceiling below. A one-story house will have either an "open-beamed" ceiling—flat or pitched—or a "finished" ceiling. In simple terms, a finished ceiling covers the roof rafters and sheathing which, if exposed, would constitute an open-beamed ceiling. With a flat roof, the finished ceiling is attached directly to the rafters. The ceiling below a pitched roof is attached to joists or to a metal or wooden frame.

Removing a partition wall

Often a major kitchen remodeling means removing all or part of an interior wall to enlarge the space.

Walls that define your kitchen may be bearing or nonbearing. A bearing wall helps support the weight of the house; a nonbearing wall does not. An interior nonbearing wall, often called a partition wall, may be removed without special precautions. The procedure outlined in this section applies to partitions only. If you're considering a remodeling project that involves moving a bearing wall or any wall beneath a second story, consult an architect or contractor about problems and procedures.

How can you tell the difference in walls? All exterior walls running perpendicular to ceiling and floor joists are bearing. Normally, at least one main interior wall is also a bearing wall. If possible, climb up into the attic or crawlspace and check the ceiling joists. If they are joined over any wall, that wall is bearing. Even if joists span the entire width of the house, their midsections may be resting on a bearing wall at the point of maximum allowable span. If you have any doubts about the wall, consult an architect, contractor, or building inspector.

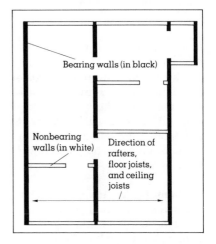

Bearing walls (in black)

Nonbearing walls (in white)

Direction of rafters, floor joists, and ceiling joists

Though removing a partition wall is not complicated, it can be quite messy. Cover the floors and furnishings, and wear a painter's mask, safety glasses, and gloves. NOTE: Check the wall for signs of electrical wiring, water and drain pipes, or heating and ventilation ducts. Any of these obstructions must be carefully rerouted before you remove the wall.

Removing wall covering. First, if there's a door in the wall, remove it from its hinges. Pry off any door trim, ceiling molding, and base molding.

The most common wall covering is gypsum wallboard nailed to wall studs. To remove it, knock holes in the wallboard with a hammer, then pull it away from the studs with a pry bar. After one surface is re-

BASIC STRUCTURAL ANATOMY

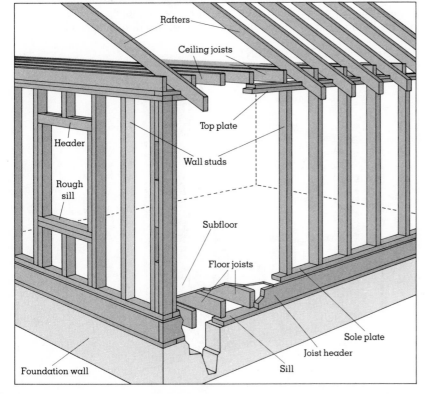

Rafters

Ceiling joists

Top plate

Header

Wall studs

Rough sill

Subfloor

Floor joists

Sole plate

Joist header

Foundation wall

Sill

... Structural basics

HOW TO REMOVE WALL FRAMING

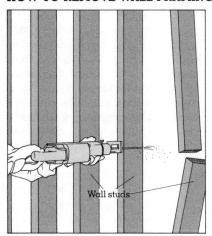

Saw through the middle of the wall studs; bend the studs sideways to free the nails from the top and sole plates.

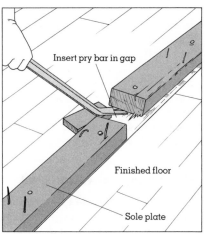

Cut gaps through the sole plate with a saw and chisel; insert a pry bar in each gap to free the sole plate.

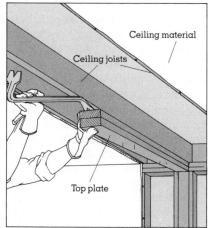

Strip ceiling materials back from the top plate, cut gaps in the plate, and pry out sections of plate.

moved, you can hit the other side from behind to knock it free.

If the wall covering is plaster and lath, chisel away the plaster until the lath backing—wood strips or metal—is exposed. You'll have to cut through the lath to break it up; then pry the lath and plaster away from the studs.

Dismantling the framing. Remove studs by sawing through the middle of each one; then, push and pull them sideways to free the nails. To get at end studs (attached to studs or nailing blocks in adjacent walls), strip wall coverings back to the bordering studs and pry loose the end stud from the side.

To remove the sole plate, saw a small section out of the middle down to the finished floor level, chisel through the remaining thickness, and insert a pry bar in the gap.

To remove a top plate that lies parallel to the joists, cut ceiling materials back to adjacent joists, and pry off the plate. If the top plate is perpendicular to the joists, cut an even 2-foot strip in the ceiling materials, making certain that you don't cut into joists; remove the plate.

Patching walls, ceilings, and floors. Wallboard and plaster aren't difficult to patch (see page 110); the real challenge lies in matching a spe-

cial texture, wallpaper, shade of paint, or well-aged floor. This is not a problem if your remodeling plans call for new wall coverings, ceiling, or flooring. In either case, see the sections on "Walls & ceilings" (pages 103–107) and "Flooring" (pages 114–119) for techniques and tips.

Framing a new wall

To separate a kitchen from an adjoining living area or to subdivide

space within the kitchen, you may need to build a new partition wall.

Framing a wall is a straightforward task, but you must measure carefully and continue to check the alignment as work progresses. The basic steps are listed below. To install a doorway, see page 86.

Plotting the location. The new wall must be anchored securely to the floor, ceiling joists, and, if possible, to wall framing on one side.

WALL FRAMING COMPONENTS

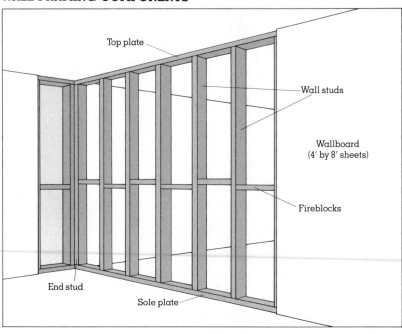

To locate the studs, try knocking with your fist along the wall until the sound changes from hollow to solid. If you have wallboard, you can use an inexpensive stud finder; often, though, the nails that hold wallboard to the studs are visible on close inspection.

To locate ceiling joists, use the same methods or, from the attic or crawlspace, drive small nails down through the ceiling on both sides of a joist to serve as reference points below. Adjacent joists and studs will be evenly spaced, usually 16 or 24 inches away from those you've located.

A wall running perpendicular to the joists will demand least effort to attach. If wall and joists will run parallel, though, try to center the wall under a single joist; otherwise, you'll need to install nailing blocks every 2 feet between two parallel joists (see illustration above right). If the side of the new wall falls between existing studs you'll need to install additional nailing blocks.

On the ceiling, mark both ends of the center line of the new wall. Measure 1¾ inches (half the width of a 2 by 4 top plate) on both sides of each mark; snap parallel lines between corresponding marks with a chalkline; the top plate will occupy the space between the lines.

Positioning the sole plate. Hang a plumb bob from each end of the lines you just marked and mark these new points on the floor. Snap two more chalklines to connect the floor points.

Cut both sole plate and top plate to the desired length. Lay the sole

HOW TO ANCHOR A TOP PLATE

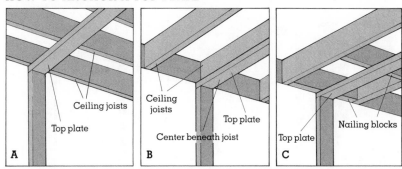

To anchor a top plate, nail to perpendicular joists (A), to the bottom of the parallel joist (B), or install nailing blocks between the parallel joists (C).

plate between the lines on the floor and nail it in place with 10-penny nails spaced every 2 feet. (If you have a masonry floor, use a masonry bit to drill holes through the sole plate every 2 or 3 feet. Then insert expansion bolts.)

If you're planning a doorway (see "Framing a doorway," page 86), don't nail through that section of the plate; it will be cut out later.

Marking stud positions. Lay the top plate against the sole plate, as shown in the illustration below. Beginning at the end that will be attached to an existing stud or to nailing blocks, measure in 1½ inches—the thickness of a 2 by 4 stud—and draw a line across both plates with a combination square. Starting once more from that end, measure and draw lines at 15¼ and 16¾ inches. From these lines, advance 16 inches at a time, drawing new lines, until the far end of both plates is reached. Each set of lines will outline the placement of a stud, with all studs

evenly spaced 16 inches "on center" (O.C.). Don't worry if the spacing at the far end is less than 16 inches. (If local codes permit, use a 24-inch spacing—you'll save lumber—and adjust the initial placement of lines to 23¼ and 24¾ inches.)

Fastening the top plate. With two helpers, lift the top plate into position between the lines (marked on the ceiling); nail it to perpendicular joists, to one parallel joist, or to nailing blocks, as shown above.

Attaching the studs. Measure and cut the studs to exact length. Attach one end stud (or both) to existing studs or to nailing blocks between studs. Lift the remaining studs into place one at a time; line them up on the marks, and check plumb with a carpenter's level. Toenail the studs to both top plate and sole plate with 8-penny nails.

Many building codes require horizontal fireblocks between studs. The number of rows depends on the code; if permitted, position blocks to provide an extra nailing surface for wall materials.

Finishing. After the studs are installed, it's time to add electrical outlets and switches (see pages 96–97), as well as new plumbing (pages 90–92). It's also time for the building inspector to check your work. Following the inspection, you can apply wall coverings of your choice (see pages 103–107), patch the ceiling, and add base moldings.

HOW TO MARK STUD POSITIONS

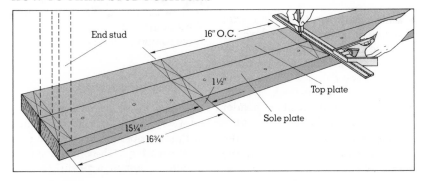

End stud   16" O.C.   1½"   Top plate   Sole plate   15¼"   16¾"

(Continued on next page)

. . . Structural basics

HOW TO FRAME A DOORWAY

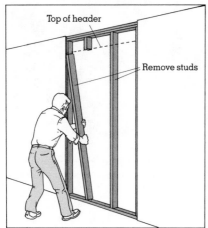

Mark and cut studs within the opening, even with the top of the new header.

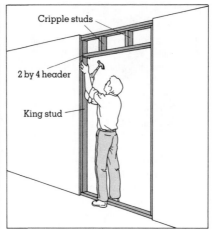

Nail the new header to the king studs; nail into ends of the new cripple studs.

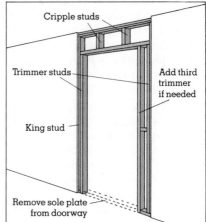

Nail trimmer studs to the king studs; block out a third trimmer, if needed.

Framing a doorway

Relocating kitchen appliances, cabinets or counters, or simply redirecting traffic flow may involve moving a door opening. Covering an existing door is relatively easy (see below). To create a new opening, it's necessary to remove wall materials, add door framing, and possibly hang a new door. Be sure the wall you plan to cut into is a nonbearing wall (see "Removing a partition wall," page 83). If the wall contains electrical wires, pipes, or ductwork, they must be rerouted.

Positioning the opening. Are you planning an open doorway, or a frame for a bifold, sliding, or standard prehung door? Determine the door type before starting work, and check the manufacturer's "rough opening" dimensions—the exact wall opening required after the new framing is in place.

You'll need to plan an opening large enough to accommodate both the rough opening and the rough door framing—an additional 1½ inches on top and sides, plus an extra ½ inch all around for shimming the typical door frame (adjusting level and plumb).

Often it's simpler to remove the wallboard from floor to ceiling between two bordering studs (the new king studs) that will remain in place. (This is the method illustrated.) In any case, you'll save work later if you can use at least one existing stud as part of the rough framing.

Regardless of the method you choose, use a carpenter's level for a straightedge, and mark the outline of the opening on the wall.

Removing wall covering and studs. First remove any base molding. Cut along the door outline with a reciprocating or keyhole saw, being careful to sever only the wallboard, not the studs beneath. Pry the wallboard away from the framing. To remove plaster and lath, chisel through the plaster to expose the lath; then cut the lath and pry it loose.

Cut the studs inside the opening to the height required for the header (see drawing above). Using a combination square, mark these studs on the face and one side, then cut carefully with a reciprocating or crosscut saw. Pry the cut studs loose from the sole plate.

Framing the opening. With wall covering and studs removed, you're ready to frame the opening. Measure and cut the header (for a partition wall you can use a 2 by 4 laid flat), and toenail it to the king studs with 8-penny nails. Nail the header to the bottoms of the cripple studs.

Cut the sole plate within the opening, and pry it away from the subfloor.

Cut trimmer studs and nail them to the king studs with 10-penny nails in a staggered pattern. You'll probably need to adjust the width by blocking out a third trimmer from one side, as shown above right. (Leave an extra ½ inch on each side for shimming if you're installing a door frame.)

Hanging the door. Bifold, swinging, or sliding pocket doors are most commonly used in kitchens. Methods of hanging doors vary considerably, depending on type. Check the manufacturer's instructions carefully before you plan the wall opening.

Even if you're not hanging a door, you'll probably want to install a preassembled door frame—consisting of a top jamb and two side jambs—to cover the rough framing.

Installing trim. When the framing is completed and the door is hung, patch the wallboard (see page 110) and install new trim (casing) around the opening. Some prehung doors have casing attached.

Closing a doorway

It's easy to eliminate an existing doorway. Simply add new studs within the opening and attach new wall coverings. The only trick is to match the present wall surface.

First, remove the casing around the opening. Then remove the door from its hinges or guide track and pry any jambs or tracks away from the rough framing.

Next, measure the gap on the floor between the existing trimmer studs; cut a length of 2 by 4 to serve as a new sole plate. Nail it to the floor with 10-penny nails. (If you have a masonry floor, attach the 2 by 4 with expansion bolts.)

Measure and cut new studs to fill the space; position one stud beneath each cripple stud. Toenail the studs to new sole plate and header with 8-penny nails. Add fireblocks between studs if required by the local code.

Strip the wall coverings back far enough to give yourself a firm nailing surface and an even edge. Then add new coverings to match the existing ones (see page 103), or resurface the entire wall. Match or replace the baseboard molding.

Window basics

Framing and hanging a window is similar to installing a door (see page 86), though in addition you must cut into the exterior siding and sheathing of the house. But the most important factor to consider is the possibility that you may be dealing with a bearing wall (see page 83). Removing studs from a bearing wall means constructing a temporary support wall before you start work and using more rigid framing than that required for partition wall openings.

An outline of basic window installation follows. For details about tools and step-by-step techniques, see the *Sunset* book *Windows & Skylights.*

Removing an existing window. First remove any interior and exterior trim that's not an integral part of the unit. Take out the sash, if possible (see drawing above); then remove the frame. The frame may have been nailed directly to the rough framing materials or secured by flanges or brackets.

BASIC WINDOW COMPONENTS

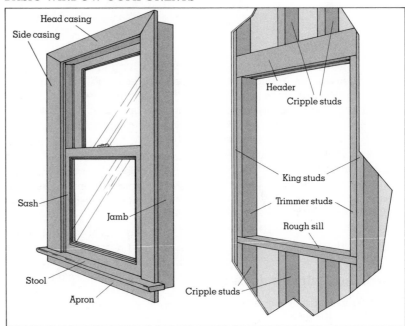

Basic window framing. Unlike rough door framing, window framing includes cripple studs at the top *and* bottom. The rough sill—a length of 2 by 4 lumber laid flat and sometimes doubled for strength—lies at the bottom edge of the opening. The top edge is bounded by the header. The header for a bearing wall opening and (depending on local codes) for any exterior wall is typically composed of matching lengths of "2-by" framing lumber turned on edge, with ½-inch-thick plywood spacers sandwiched between them. The exact size of 2-by material required depends on both the width of the window opening and your local building code.

Cutting a new opening. You'll receive a rough opening size for your new window from the manufacturer. The actual opening will be somewhat larger: add to the rough opening size the dimensions of the king studs, trimmer studs, header, and sill, plus an extra ⅜ inch on all sides for leveling and plumbing the window. Work from the inside of the house outward. If possible, complete the rough framing before opening the siding to the elements.

Installing a prehung window. A prehung window arrives with the sash already installed inside the window frame—and frequently with the exterior casing (trim) attached. To simply replace an existing window with another of the same size, first remove the interior trim and measure the rough opening; then order the new window to fit.

Using wood shims or blocks, center, level, and plumb the new window in the opening; then fasten it to the rough framing. Depending on window type, you'll either nail through a flange into the outside sheathing, screw the jambs to the header and trimmer studs, or nail through preassembled exterior trim.

Finishing touches. Your new window may need exterior casing and a drip cap. Or you may be required to install metal flashing over the unit's top edge. Thoroughly caulk the joints between the siding and the new window.

Cover the top and sides of the inside opening with casing and install a finished stool over the rough sill. Finally, add one last strip of casing (called an apron).

(Continued on page 89)

AN INTRODUCTION TO GREENHOUSE WINDOWS

Like its full-scale counterpart, a greenhouse window addition will nurture as well as showcase your favorite plants. The greenhouse window also provides a unique decorating tool: plant-laden shelves reach beyond a wall and seemingly expand an enclosed room into the open space beyond. Extending a kitchen countertop into the window unit heightens this illusion; it also can bring within reach an herb garden to inspire a cook.

Greenhouse window details

Greenhouse windows range from 3 feet square to 10 feet wide and 5 feet tall. (Units wider than 5 feet may require special framing and installation.) Standard depth is 12 to 16 inches. Preassembled units include glazing, framing, and adjustable shelving.

Choose either glass or plastic glazing; both offer a variety of finishes. Though plastic is shatter-resistant, glass is more durable and less prone to scratching. Aluminum structural sections are lightweight and maintenance-free; wood-framed units, though bulkier, offer you greater possibility in the choice of finish.

Options in greenhouse units include weatherstripping along vents to decrease cold air infiltration, screening inside vents to keep insects out, and double glazing to slow heat loss.

Other means of controlling heat loss through a greenhouse window include interior shutters and quilted window covers that isolate the unit from heated living space. For further information on insulating and shading windows, refer to the *Sunset* book *Windows & Skylights*.

Installing the window unit

Installation techniques differ, depending on local building codes, the exterior siding of your house, type of window unit, and whether or not you're replacing an existing window with a unit of the same size. Greenhouse windows can be attached to the wall around an existing opening or to an existing wooden frame.

Before purchasing a window unit, it's a good idea to study various manufacturers' specifications and installation instructions.

Adding furring strips. If your home has a wood-finished exterior such as beveled siding or shingles, you'll need to add 1 by 4 furring strips around the window frame. (For masonry, masonry veneer, or stucco, follow the manufacturers' instructions or consult a contractor.)

To attach the strips, cut the siding back to the underlying sheathing so that the furring can lie flat. If building paper covers the sheathing, leave the paper intact.

Apply a generous bed of caulking to the sheathing or building paper. Then secure the furring with nails long enough to penetrate furring, building paper, and sheathing. Nails should extend into the studs or header a distance equal to twice the thickness of the furring. Set the nail heads below the furring surface.

Mounting the greenhouse window. With helpers holding the unit in place, level the window. Temporarily nail the unit in place and check the level again. Attach the window unit with screws long enough to penetrate the mounting flange, furring, sheathing, building paper, and at least an inch into the studs and header.

Finishing details. For units wider than 5 feet, bracing between the base and wall is recommended. Caulk the seams between the flange and furring and between the furring and siding. If you like, you can cover the base of the window with tile or finish it to match an adjacent countertop.

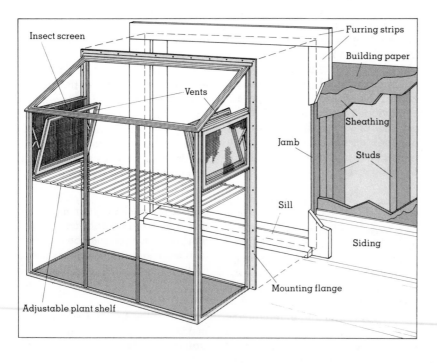

Insect screen · Vents · Adjustable plant shelf · Jamb · Sill · Mounting flange · Furring strips · Building paper · Sheathing · Studs · Siding

.. Structural basics

Skylight basics

Installing a skylight in a pitched roof with asphalt or wood shingles is a two-part process: you cut and frame openings in both roof and ceiling, and connect the two openings with a vertical or angled light shaft. (You don't even need a light shaft for a flat roof or open-beamed ceiling, which requires only a single opening.) A brief description of the skylight installation sequence follows; for a complete discussion of required techniques and tools, see the *Sunset* book *Windows & Skylights*.

Marking the openings. Using the rough opening measurements supplied by the manufacturer, mark the location of the ceiling opening; then drive nails up through the four corners and center so they'll be visible in the attic or crawlspace. From the attic, check for obstructions, shifting the location if necessary. You'll save work if you can use one or two ceiling joists as the edges of your opening.

With a plumb bob, transfer the ceiling marks to the underside of the roof; again, drive nails up through the roofing materials to mark the location. If you run into obstructions on the roof, change the position slightly and use an angled light shaft to connect the two openings.

Framing the roof opening. On a day with zero probability of rain, cut and frame the roof opening. Exercise extreme caution when working on the roof; if the pitch is steep or if you have a tile or slate roof, you might consider leaving this part to professionals.

When you work with a skylight designed to be mounted on a curb frame, build the curb first; 2 by 6 lumber is commonly used. (If your skylight has an integral curb or is self-flashing, you can skip this step.)

To determine the actual size of the opening you need to cut, add the dimensions of any framing materials (see below) to the rough opening size marked by the nails. You may need to remove some extra shingles

BASIC SKYLIGHT COMPONENTS

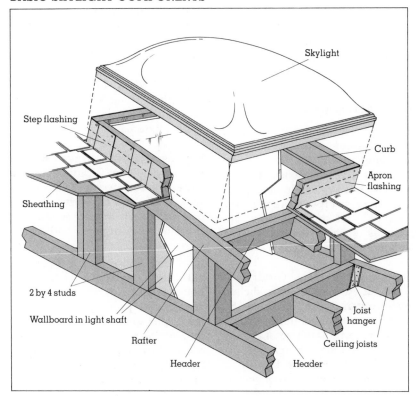

Skylight

Step flashing

Curb

Apron flashing

Sheathing

2 by 4 studs

Wallboard in light shaft

Rafter

Joist hanger

Ceiling joists

Header

Header

or roofing materials down to the sheathing to accommodate the flashing of a curb-mounted unit or the flange of a self-flashing unit.

Cut the roof opening in successive layers: roofing materials first, sheathing next, and finally any necessary rafters. Before cutting the rafters, support them by 2 by 4s nailed to the ceiling joists below.

To frame the opening, you'll need double headers and possibly trimmers. Install the headers with double joist hangers.

If you're installing a curb-mounted unit, position and flash the curb. Toenail the curb to the rafters or trimmers and to the headers. Pay special attention to the manufacturer's instructions concerning directions for flashing.

Mounting the skylight. For a curb-mounted unit, secure the skylight to the top of the curb with nails and a sealant. Set a self-flashing unit in roofing cement, then nail through the flange directly to the roof sheathing. Coat the joints and nail holes with more roofing cement.

Opening the ceiling. Double-check your original ceiling marks against the roof opening and the intended angle of the light shaft. Cut through the ceiling materials and then sever the joists. Support joists to be cut— do this by bracing them against adjacent joists. Frame the opening in the same manner used for the roof opening.

Building a light shaft. Measure the distance between the ceiling headers and roof headers at each corner and at 16-inch intervals between the corners. Cut studs to fit the measurements and install them as illustrated above. This provides a nailing surface for wall coverings.

Final touches. Insulate the spaces between studs in the light shaft before fastening wall coverings to the studs. Painting wallboard white maximizes reflected light.

Trim the ceiling opening with molding strips. Adding a plastic ceiling panel (either manufactured or cut to size) helps diffuse light evenly.

Plumbing basics

Do you know how your plumbing system works? If not, the kitchen is a good place to start learning, for the plumbing here is much less complicated than in other areas—bathrooms, for instance.

A plumbing overview

Three complementary sets of pipes work together to fill your home's plumbing needs: the drain-waste and vent (DWV) systems, and the water supply system. In the typical kitchen, these pipes serve the "sink complex"—the sink and related appliances, such as the dishwasher and garbage disposer.

The supply system. Water that eventually arrives at your kitchen faucet enters the house from the public water main or from a source on the property. At the water service entrance, the main supply line divides in two—one line branching off to be heated by the water heater,

the other remaining as cold water. The two pipes usually run parallel below the first-floor level until they reach the vicinity of a group of fixtures, then head up through the wall or floor. Sometimes the water supply—hot, cold, or both—passes through a water softener or filter (see drawing below) before reaching the fixtures.

Drain-waste and vent systems. The drain-waste pipes channel waste water and solid wastes to the sewer line. Vent pipes carry away sewer gas and maintain atmospheric pressure in drainpipes and fixture traps.

Every house has a main soil stack that serves a dual function: below the level of the fixtures, it is your home's primary drainpipe; at its upper end, which protrudes through the roof, the stack becomes a vent. Drainpipes from individual fixtures, as well as larger branch drains, connect to the main stack. A

fixture or fixture group located on a branch drain far from the main stack will have a secondary vent stack of its own rising to the roof.

The sink complex. Generally, a single set of vertical supply pipes and one drainpipe serve the entire kitchen. For both convenience and economy, fixtures and appliances that require water usually are adjacent to the sink. Supply pipes for a dishwasher, hot water dispenser, and automatic ice maker branch off the main hot and cold supply lines leading to the sink faucet. Similarly, the dishwasher and disposer share the sink's trap and drainpipe. The hot water dispenser discharges directly into the sink.

Roughing-in new plumbing

You will need to add new plumbing to your kitchen if you move your present sink and related appliances, plumb a sink into a new

A PLUMBING OVERVIEW

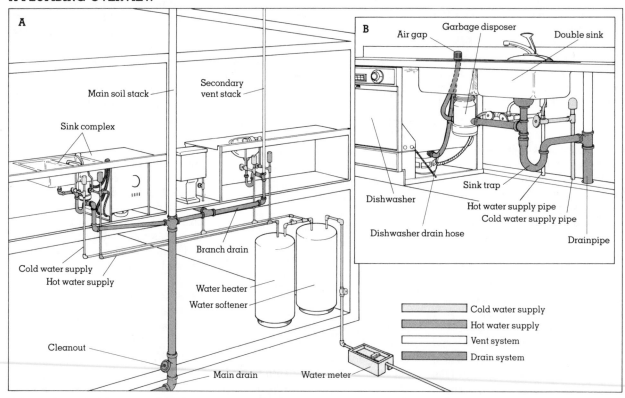

Your kitchen's plumbing is part of a coordinated system of hot and cold supply pipes leading water to fixtures and appliances, and drain-waste and vent pipes carrying wastes and gases away (A). Kitchen plumbing is commonly concentrated in the "sink complex" area (B).

kitchen island, or add a new fixture—such as a second sink.

For basic pipefitting techniques, refer to the *Sunset* book *Basic Plumbing Illustrated*. With a little experience, you may be able to handle these jobs yourself. If you have doubts about your abilities, consider hiring a professional to rough-in the new pipes. By referring to pages 120–127, you can hook up the fixtures or appliances.

Mapping your present system. If you're considering a plumbing change, you'll first need a detailed map of the present plumbing. Begin your investigation from an unfinished basement or crawlspace or, if necessary, from the attic or roof. Locate the main stack, branch drains, and any secondary stacks. Positioning yourself directly below or above the kitchen, try to determine whether the sink complex is tied directly into the main stack or connected to a branch drain with its own vent. Find the spot where vertical supply lines branch off from horizontal lines and head up into a wall or the floor.

Extending DWV pipes. Your plans to relocate a sink or add a new fixture depend on the feasibility of extending present DWV pipes. Plumbing codes, both national and local, are quite specific about the following: the size of the drainpipe or

branch drain serving the kitchen sink complex or any new fixture requiring drainage; the distance (called the "critical distance") from the traps to the main stack, secondary stack, or other vent; and the point where a new drainpipe or branch drain ties into the branch drain or main stack.

A proposed fixture located within a few feet of the main stack (check local codes for the exact distance) usually can be drained and vented directly by the stack. New fixtures distant from the stack probably will require a new branch drain beneath the floor, running either to the stack or to an existing cleanout in the main drain (see drawing below); you'll also need to run a new secondary stack up to the roof.

The drainpipe required for a kitchen sink complex normally has a diameter of at least 1½ inches (2 inches if you also plan to vent directly into the stack). Minimum vent size for a secondary stack is commonly 1¼ inches, unless a dishwasher installed without a separate air gap necessitates a larger pipe.

Your present DWV pipes probably are made of cast iron, with "hub" or "bell-and-spigot" ends joined by molten lead and oakum. To extend the system, you may substitute "hubless" fittings (consisting of neoprene gaskets and stainless steel clamps), which are simpler to install.

Since plastic is considerably lighter than cast iron and is easily joined with solvent cement, you may want to use ABS (acrylonitrile-butadiene-styrene) or PVC (polyvinyl chloride) pipe in your extension. First check the local code; many areas prohibit the use of plastic pipe.

Extending supply pipes. Because no venting is required, extending sup-

PIPES & FITTINGS

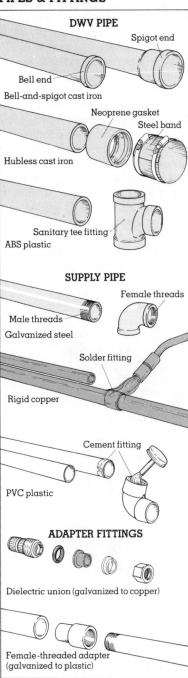

DWV PIPE

Spigot end

Bell end
Bell-and-spigot cast iron

Neoprene gasket
Steel band

Hubless cast iron

Sanitary tee fitting
ABS plastic

SUPPLY PIPE

Female threads

Male threads
Galvanized steel

Solder fitting

Rigid copper

Cement fitting

PVC plastic

ADAPTER FITTINGS

Dielectric union (galvanized to copper)

Female-threaded adapter
(galvanized to plastic)

HOW TO EXTEND YOUR PLUMBING SYSTEM

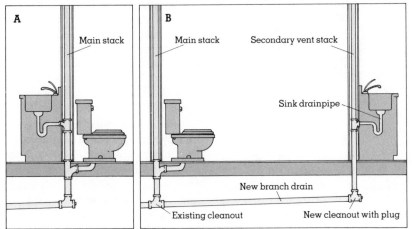

A

Main stack

B

Main stack

Secondary vent stack

Sink drainpipe

New branch drain

Existing cleanout

New cleanout with plug

To drain kitchen plumbing additions, you can either (A) tap into the present main stack, if nearby, or (B) install a new branch drain and secondary vent stack.

. . . Plumbing basics

ply pipes is a much easier task than extending the DWV system. The selection of correctly sized pipes, as outlined in detail by local codes, depends equally on the type of fixture to be added, the volume of water it demands, and the length of the new pipe.

Your home's supply pipes most likely are either galvanized steel (referred to as "galvanized" or "iron" pipe) connected by threaded fittings, or rigid copper joined with soldered fittings. Some local codes permit the use of plastic supply lines; special adapters will enable you to convert from one material to another (see page 91).

Routing new pipes. Ideally, new drainpipes should be routed below the kitchen floor. They can be suspended from floor joists by pipe hangers, inserted in the space between parallel joists, or threaded through notches or holes drilled in perpendicular joists. If you have a finished basement, you'll need to cut into the ceiling to thread pipes between or through joists, hide the pipes with a dropped ceiling, or box them in.

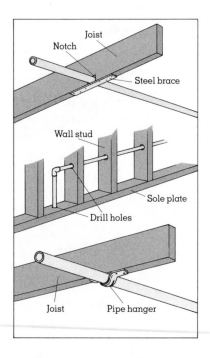

Drainpipes must slope away from fixtures; a minimum slope of ¼ inch per foot is usually required.

A new vent stack must be installed inside an existing wall (a big job), built into a new or "thickened" wall (see "Building a wet wall," below), or concealed in a closet or cabinet. In mild climates, an enclosed vent may also run up the exterior of the house, within a box.

Supply pipes normally follow drainpipes, but for convenience, can be routed directly up through the wall or floor from main horizontal lines below. Supply pipes should run parallel to each other, at least 6 inches apart.

Building a wet wall. The main soil stack, and often a secondary stack, are commonly hidden inside an oversize house wall called a "wet wall."

Unlike an ordinary 2 by 4 stud wall (shown on page 84), a wet wall has a sole plate and top plate built from 2 by 6 or 2 by 8 lumber. Additionally, the 2 by 4 studs are set in pairs, on edge, as shown below. This construction creates maximum space inside the wall for large DWV pipes (which often are wider than a standard wall) and for the fittings which are wider yet.

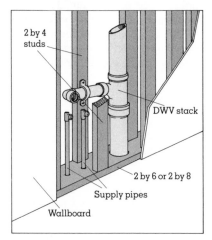

You can also "fur out" an existing wall to hide added pipes—attach new 2 by 4s to the old ones, then add new wall coverings (see above right). Similarly, a new branch drain that can't run below the floor may be hidden by furring strips laid beside the pipe and covered with

new flooring materials. (For flooring details, see pages 114–119.)

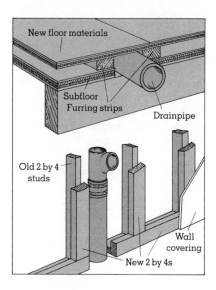

Gas system basics

When you convert from electricity to gas or simply relocate a gas appliance, keep in mind a few basic guidelines.

Materials approved for gas supply vary with the area and the type of gas. The most universally accepted materials are threaded pipe of galvanized steel, and "black pipe" (steel pipe without galvanizing). Heavier grades of copper pipe used for plumbing systems (types K and L) are also permitted in some areas.

The plumbing code, or separate gas code, will specify pipe size according to cubic foot capacity and the length of pipe between the meter or storage tank and the appliance. All gas appliances should have a numerical rating in BTUs per hour stamped on the nameplate. To convert BTUs to cubic feet, figure 1,000 BTUs to 1 cubic foot; for example, 65,000 BTUs = 65 cubic feet.

Each appliance must have a nearby code-approved shutoff valve with a straight handle, to turn off gas in an emergency.

There's no room for error when installing a gas system. It's advisable to have a professional make the installation. You must, in any case, have the work inspected and tested before the gas is turned on.

Electrical basics

What may appear to be a hopelessly tangled maze of wires running through the walls and ceiling of your home is actually a well-organized system of circuits. In your kitchen, those circuits serve the light fixtures, switches, and power outlets. Some circuits run directly to large appliances.

This section explains the electrical system in relation to kitchen lighting and appliances, and offers techniques for basic electrical improvements. More detailed step-by-step instructions may be found in the *Sunset* book *Basic Home Wiring Illustrated*. For details on installing light fixtures, see pages 98–102.

Should you do your own electrical work? It's not always permitted. Local building departments restrict the extent and type of new wiring a homeowner may undertake. In some areas, for example, you may not be permitted to add a new circuit to the service panel. Or if the wiring inside the walls of an older home is the knob-and-tube variety, local regulations may require that new hookups be made by licensed electricians. When restrictions don't apply, problems can still crop up. If you have any doubt about how to proceed, it's best to hire a professional.

Before you do any of the work yourself, talk with your building department's electrical inspector about local codes, the National Electrical Code (NEC), and your area's requirements concerning permits and inspections.

Understanding your system

Today most homes have what's called "three-wire" service. The utility company connects three wires to your service entrance panel. Each of two "hot" wires supplies electricity at approximately 120 volts. During normal operation, the third—or "neutral"—wire is maintained at zero volts. (Don't be misled, though, by the harmless sound of "neutral"; all three wires are "live.")

Three-wire service provides both 120-volt and 240-volt capabilities. One hot wire and the neutral wire combine to supply 120 volts, used for most household applications such as lights and small appliances. Both hot wires and the neutral wire can complete a 120/240-volt circuit for such needs as an electric range or clothes dryer.

Many older homes have only two-wire service, with one hot wire at 120 volts and one neutral wire. Two-wire service does not have 240-volt capability.

Service entrance panel. This panel is the control center for your electrical system. Inside you'll find the main disconnect (main fuses or main circuit breaker), the fuses or circuit breakers protecting individual circuits, and the grounding connection for the entire system.

After entering the panel and passing through the main disconnect, each hot wire connects to one of two "bus bars," as shown below. These bars accept the amount of current permitted by the main disconnect and allow you to divide that current into smaller branch circuits. The neutral wire is attached to a neutral bus bar, which is in direct contact with the earth through the grounding electrode conductor.

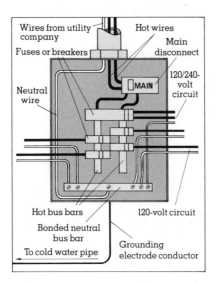

Wires from utility company · Hot wires · Main disconnect · Fuses or breakers · MAIN · 120/240-volt circuit · Neutral wire · Hot bus bars · 120-volt circuit · Bonded neutral bus bar · Grounding electrode conductor · To cold water pipe

Your home may also have one or more subpanels from which branch circuits originate. A subpanel is an extension of the service entrance panel; the two are connected by hot and neutral "subfeeds."

Simple circuitry. The word "circuit" represents the course that electric current travels; carried by the hot wire, it passes from the service entrance panel or subpanel to one or more devices using electricity (such as a group of light fixtures), then returns to the panel by way of the neutral wire. The devices are normally connected by parallel wiring, as shown below. The hot and neutral wires run continuously from one fixture or outlet box to another; separate wires branch off to individual devices.

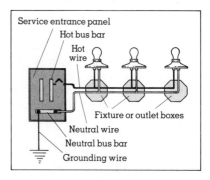

Service entrance panel · Hot bus bar · Hot wire · Fixture or outlet boxes · Neutral wire · Neutral bus bar · Grounding wire

Each 120-volt branch circuit consists of one hot wire and one neutral wire. The hot wire originates at a branch circuit fuse or circuit breaker connected to one of the hot bus bars. A 120/240-volt circuit, which requires both hot wires, is connected through the fuse or breaker to both hot bus bars. All neutral conductors originate at the neutral bus bar inside the panel.

Grounding prevents shock. The NEC requires that every circuit have a grounding system. Grounding ensures that all metal parts of a wiring system will be maintained at zero volts. In the event of a short circuit, a grounding wire carries current back to the service entrance panel and ensures that the fuse or circuit breaker will open, shutting off the flow of current.

The grounding wire for each circuit is attached to the neutral bus bar and then is run with the hot and neutral wires; individual "jumper" wires branch off to ground individual metal devices and boxes as required.

(Continued on next page)

... Electrical basics

Planning electrical improvements

Before you start daydreaming about new track lighting, a dishwasher, or a disposer, you'll need to know whether your present system can handle an additional load.

Service type and rating. First, determine your present type of electrical service. Looking through the window of your meter, you'll see several numbers on the faceplate: 120V indicates two-wire service; 240V indicates three-wire service that provides both 120-volt and 240-volt capabilities.

Your electrical system is also rated for the maximum amount of current (measured in amperes—or "amps") it can carry. This "service rating," determined by the size of the service entrance equipment, should be stamped on the main fuses or circuit breaker. If your system doesn't have a main disconnect, call your utility company or building department for the rating.

Codes. Requirements for electrical circuits serving a modern kitchen and dining area are clearly prescribed by the NEC. Plug-in outlets and switches for small appliances

and the refrigerator must be served by a minimum of two 20-amp circuits. Light fixtures are not connected to these circuits, but they share one or more 15-amp circuits. These latter circuits also run, as a rule, to the dining room, living room, or other adjacent space.

If you're installing a dishwasher and/or disposer, you'll need a separate 20-amp circuit for each. Most electric ranges use an individual 50-amp, 120/240-volt major appliance circuit. Wall ovens and a separate cooktop may share a 50-amp circuit.

Tapping into a present circuit. A circuit can be tapped wherever there's an accessible housing box (see "Selecting a power source," page 95). Because of code restrictions, though, you must tap the correct *type* of circuit.

You also must determine that the circuit you hope to tap doesn't already carry the maximum load allowed. For help in mapping your circuits, consult an electrician, your building department, or the *Sunset* book *Basic Home Wiring Illustrated*.

Adding a new circuit. When an existing circuit can't handle a new load

or when a new appliance requires its own circuit, you can often add a new circuit or a subpanel. However, your present house load combined with the proposed addition still must not exceed your service rating.

To help calculate the house load, the NEC has established representative values and formulas based on typical electrical usage. For further aid check with your building department's electrical inspector.

Older homes with two-wire service of less than 100 amps simply can't support many major improvements. To add a new oven or dishwasher you may need to increase your service type and rating, which means replacing the service entrance equipment.

Working with wire

To wire basic extensions to your present electrical circuits, you'll need a few tools and materials, a knack for making wire splices, and the patience to route new wire from box to box and then patch wall and ceiling materials. For work on this scale, an electrical permit will probably be required.

Here's the most important rule for all do-it-yourself electricians:

TYPICAL KITCHEN CIRCUITS

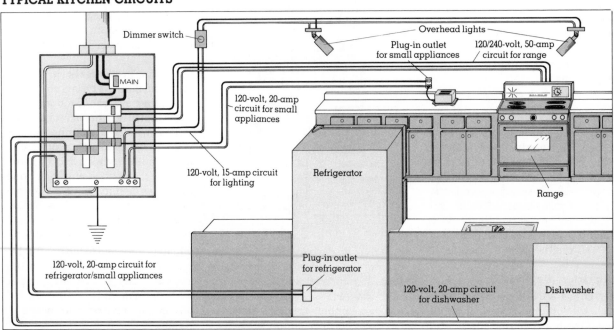

Dimmer switch

Overhead lights

Plug-in outlet for small appliances

120/240-volt, 50-amp circuit for range

MAIN

120-volt, 20-amp circuit for small appliances

120-volt, 15-amp circuit for lighting

Refrigerator

Range

120-volt, 20-amp circuit for refrigerator/small appliances

Plug-in outlet for refrigerator

120-volt, 20-amp circuit for dishwasher

Dishwasher

Never work on any "live" circuit, fixture, plug-in outlet, or switch. Your life may depend on it.

Before starting to work, you must disconnect the circuit at its source, either in the service entrance panel or in a separate subpanel. If fuses protect your circuits, remove the appropriate fuse. In a panel or subpanel equipped with circuit breakers, switch the breaker to the *OFF* position to disconnect the circuit, then tape over the switch for extra safety.

Selecting a power source. A circuit can be extended from a present outlet box, fixture box, switch box, or junction box. The one exception is a switch box without a neutral wire (see pages 96–97).

Before deciding which box to tap, consider how you'll route wire to the new switch, outlet, or fixture. Look for the easiest paths behind walls, above ceilings, and under floors. Then choose the most convenient power source.

The box tapped must be large enough to accommodate the new wires (minimum box sizes are specified by the NEC) and must have a knockout hole through which you can thread the cable. If your box doesn't meet these requirements, replace it with one that does.

Preparing for new boxes. Housing boxes—capped with fixture canopies, outlet plates, or switch plates—come in many shapes and sizes. For outlets, switches, and fixtures weighing 5 pounds or less, choose "cut-in" boxes, which need not be secured to studs or joists. (If wall or ceiling coverings haven't been in-

stalled, you can nail a "flange" box to studs or joists.) Unless codes prohibit the use of plastic, you may select either plastic or metal boxes. Metal boxes, though sturdier, must be grounded; plastic boxes cost less and need not be grounded.

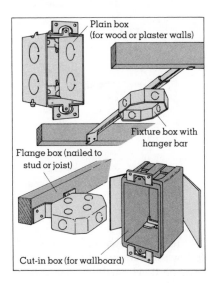

Plain box (for wood or plaster walls)

Fixture box with hanger bar

Flange box (nailed to stud or joist)

Cut-in box (for wallboard)

Position the box between studs or joists in an area free of pipes and other wires. To find a suitable location, first cut off power to all circuits that might run behind the wall or ceiling where you're placing the box. Drill a small test hole, and probe behind the surface with a length of stiff wire until you find a space.

Trace the outline of the box on the wall or ceiling, omitting any protruding brackets. Drill a starter hole in one corner, then make the cutout with a keyhole or saber saw.

Routing new cable. Your new "wires" actually will be self-contained lengths of nonmetallic sheathed ca-

ble. A single cable contains either one or two hot wires, a neutral wire, and a grounding wire, each wrapped in its own insulation. To insure the best splices, use only cable containing all-copper wire. Check local codes for the correct cable size.

After cutting the holes but before mounting the boxes, you must run cable from the power source to each new box location. Access from an unfinished basement, an unfloored attic, or a garage adjacent to the kitchen makes it easy to run cable either on top of joists and studs or through holes drilled in them.

If walls and ceilings are covered on both sides, you'll have to "fish" the cable (see drawing below). Use a fish tape (buy it at a plumbing supply or hardware store—or you may find one to rent) or a length of stiff wire.

Attaching new boxes. After you've routed the new cable, secure each housing box to the ceiling or wall. Slip a cable connector onto the end of the cable and insert it through a knockout in the box. Fasten the connector to the box, leaving 6 to 8 inches of cable free for making the connections. Then mount the box.

(Continued on next page)

HOW TO ROUTE CABLE TO FIXTURES

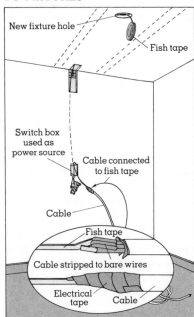

New fixture hole

Fish tape

Switch box used as power source

Cable connected to fish tape

Cable

Fish tape

Cable stripped to bare wires

Electrical tape

Cable

HOW TO ROUTE CABLE TO OUTLETS

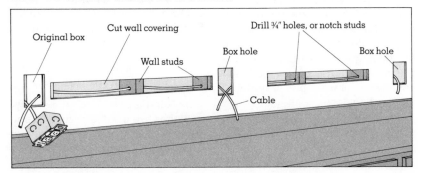

Original box

Cut wall covering

Wall studs

Drill ¾" holes, or notch studs

Box hole

Box hole

Cable

... Electrical basics

HOW TO WIRE INTO THE POWER SOURCE

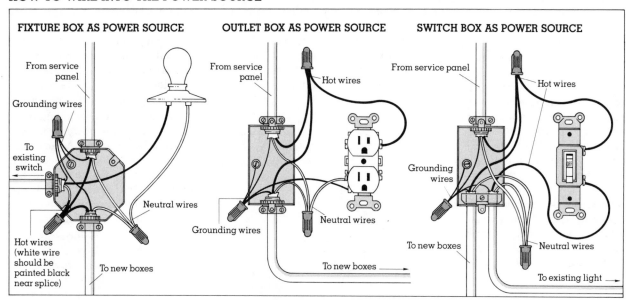

FIXTURE BOX AS POWER SOURCE

From service panel

Grounding wires

To existing switch

Hot wires (white wire should be painted black near splice)

To new boxes

Neutral wires

OUTLET BOX AS POWER SOURCE

From service panel

Hot wires

Grounding wires

Neutral wires

To new boxes

SWITCH BOX AS POWER SOURCE

From service panel

Hot wires

Grounding wires

To new boxes

Neutral wires

To existing light

Wiring into the power source. Connections to three types of boxes used as power sources are illustrated above. A fourth option is a junction box, where wires are simply joined.

Wirenuts join and protect the stripped ends of spliced wires within housing boxes. The correct wirenut size depends on the number and size of wires you'll be joining.

NOTE: For simplicity's sake, the wires illustrated on these pages are color-coded as follows:

• Hot wires: thick black or gold.

• Neutral wires: thick white.

• Grounding wires: narrow black.

Actual hot wires are usually black or red, but may be any color other than white, gray, or green. Actual neutral wires are white or gray; grounding wires are bare copper or aluminum, green, or, in rare cases, black.

Occasionally a white wire will be used as a hot wire, in which case it should be taped or painted black near terminals and splices for easy identification.

To join wires with a wirenut, follow this sequence: (A) strip 1 inch of insulation from the wire ends, and twist the ends clockwise 1½ turns; (B) snip ⅜ to ½ inch off the twisted wires; then (C) screw the wirenut clockwise onto the wires.

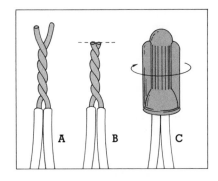

A   B   C

Wiring plug-in outlets

Plug-in outlets can be wired in several ways. You may want to keep one or both halves electrically live at all times so that appliances can be controlled by their own switches. Or you may wish to turn one or both halves on and off with wall switches—for example, to control a garbage disposer.

Outlets should be evenly distributed between small appliance circuits in the kitchen area. For example, if there are two small appliance circuits and eight outlets in the area, each circuit should serve four outlets.

All outlets for 15 or 20-amp circuits must be of the grounding type shown at the top of page 97. Outlets are rated for a specific amperage and voltage; be sure to buy the type you need.

If you want to add a grounded outlet to a circuit that does not contain a grounding wire, you'll have to run a separate wire from the new outlet to a nearby cold water pipe (see page 98). Check the neutral bus bar at the service entrance panel to find out whether the circuit has a grounding wire.

The drawings at the top of page 97 show two common ways to wire new outlets. The housing boxes are assumed to be metal; if you choose plastic, there's no need to ground the boxes, but you'll have to attach a grounding wire to each outlet. Simply loop the end of the wire under the grounding screw.

Wiring new switches

Both "single-pole" and "three-way" switches are used in homes. A single-pole switch may control one or more light fixtures or outlets; two three-way switches in different lo-

HOW TO WIRE PLUG-IN OUTLETS

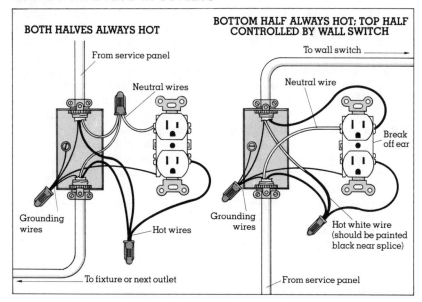

BOTH HALVES ALWAYS HOT

From service panel

Neutral wires

Grounding wires

Hot wires

To fixture or next outlet

BOTTOM HALF ALWAYS HOT; TOP HALF CONTROLLED BY WALL SWITCH

To wall switch

Neutral wire

Break off ear

Grounding wires

Hot white wire (should be painted black near splice)

From service panel

cations may also control one or more fixtures or outlets.

Like outlets, each switch must have the same amp and voltage rating as the circuit. Remember when wiring that *switches are installed only along hot wires.*

The switches shown on this page have no grounding wires. Because the plastic toggles used on most home switches are shockproof, these switches don't need to be grounded. If switches are housed inside metal boxes, the boxes *do* need to be

grounded. When installing a plastic switch box at the end of a circuit, secure the end of the grounding wire between the switch bracket and the mounting screw.

Single-pole switches. These switches have two screw terminals of the same color (usually brass) for wire connections, and a definite vertical orientation. You should be able to read the words ON and OFF embossed on the toggle. It makes no difference which hot wire goes to

which terminal. Because of code limitations on the number of wires that a switch box may contain, the cable sometimes must run to the fixture first and at other times to the switch. Check your local codes.

Three-way switches. These switches have two screw terminals of the same color (brass or silver) and one of a darker color, identified by the word "common." Either end of a three-way switch can go up. It's important to observe, though, which terminal is the odd-colored one; it may be located differently than in the drawing below.

To wire a pair of three-way switches, first connect the hot wire from the service entrance panel or subpanel to the odd-colored terminal of one switch; then connect the hot wire from the fixture or outlet to the odd-colored terminal of the other switch. Wire the remaining terminals by running hot wires from the two same-colored terminals on one switch to the two same-colored terminals on the other.

HOW TO WIRE THREE-WAY SWITCHES

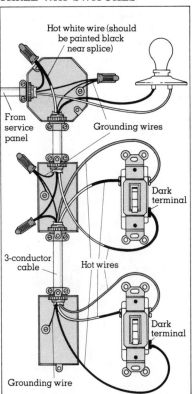

Hot white wire (should be painted black near splice)

From service panel

Grounding wires

Dark terminal

3-conductor cable

Hot wires

Dark terminal

Grounding wire

HOW TO WIRE SINGLE-POLE SWITCHES

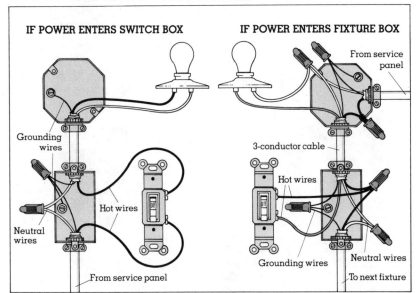

IF POWER ENTERS SWITCH BOX

Grounding wires

Hot wires

Neutral wires

From service panel

IF POWER ENTERS FIXTURE BOX

From service panel

3-conductor cable

Hot wires

Neutral wires

Grounding wires

To next fixture

Light fixtures

Kitchen lighting needs fall into two categories—general and task lighting. Both incandescent and fluorescent lights can be used to satisfy either need. You'll probably implement lighting with one or more of the three popular types of fixtures: surface-mounted, track, and recessed downlight or panel.

Replacing an existing light fixture with one of the same type usually is a minor operation; you simply unscrew the fixture from its housing box, disconnect the wires of the old fixture, and hook up new wires. Adding a new fixture where there was none is a more complex process. After running new cable from a power source, you must install a housing box and a switch to control the fixture. Do you feel that's out of your league? For help, see "Electrical basics" on pages 93–97.

Normally, you won't need an electrical permit to simply exchange fixtures or switches. You may need a permit and professional help for a new installation.

Installing surface-mounted fixtures

Surface-mounted fixtures are either attached directly to a fixture box in the wall or ceiling or suspended from the box by chains or cord. New fixtures usually come with their own mounting hardware, adaptable to any existing fixture box. Sometimes, though, the weight of the new fixture or the wiring necessary for proper grounding requires that you replace the box before installing the fixture.

Attaching fixtures. The weight of the fixture determines how it will be attached. Boxes for fixtures weighing more than 5 pounds must be nailed to a joist or hung on a bar between joists. If the fixture weighs more than 30 pounds, the fixture should be connected to the box's metallic stud with a hickey or reducing nut.

Grounding metal fixtures. The National Electrical Code requires that all incandescent and fluorescent fixtures with exposed metal parts be grounded.

If the fixture box itself is grounded (see below), the nipple or screws holding the fixture to the box will ground the fixture. There's one exception: a cord or chain-hung fixture needs a grounding wire run from the socket to the box, as shown below. Most new fixtures are prewired with a grounding wire.

If the fixture box is not grounded (as is the case when your present house wiring includes no grounding wire), you'll have to extend a grounding wire from the box to the nearest cold water pipe. To do this, you'll need a length of bare #12 copper wire, a grounding strap, and enough patience to route the wire so that it won't be an eyesore. Wrap one end of the wire around the grounding screw or around the nipple or screw holding the fixture to the box, and secure the other end to the screw that holds the strap to the pipe.

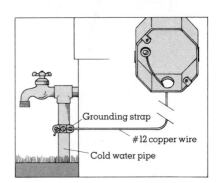

Grounding strap
#12 copper wire
Cold water pipe

Replacing fixtures. Whether you're replacing an old fixture with the same type or with a new fluorescent unit, the steps are the same.

First, disconnect the circuit by removing the fuse or switching the circuit breaker to OFF. Carefully remove the glass shade, if any, from the old fixture. Unscrew the canopy

SURFACE-MOUNTED FIXTURES

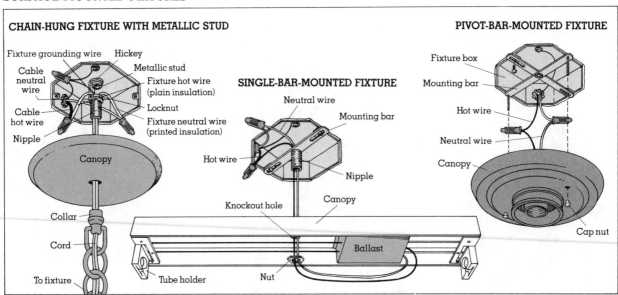

CHAIN-HUNG FIXTURE WITH METALLIC STUD

Fixture grounding wire
Hickey
Cable neutral wire
Metallic stud
Fixture hot wire (plain insulation)
Cable hot wire
Locknut
Fixture neutral wire (printed insulation)
Nipple
Canopy
Collar
Cord
To fixture

SINGLE-BAR-MOUNTED FIXTURE

Neutral wire
Mounting bar
Hot wire
Nipple
Knockout hole
Canopy
Tube holder
Nut
Ballast

PIVOT-BAR-MOUNTED FIXTURE

Fixture box
Mounting bar
Hot wire
Neutral wire
Canopy
Cap nut

TRACK SYSTEMS

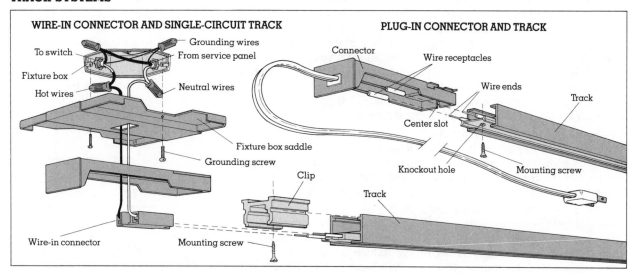

WIRE-IN CONNECTOR AND SINGLE-CIRCUIT TRACK

To switch
Grounding wires
From service panel
Fixture box
Neutral wires
Hot wires
Fixture box saddle
Grounding screw
Wire-in connector
Mounting screw

PLUG-IN CONNECTOR AND TRACK

Connector
Wire receptacles
Wire ends
Track
Center slot
Knockout hole
Mounting screw
Clip
Track

from the fixture box; detach the mounting bar if there is one. Have a helper hold the fixture to keep it from falling.

Now, make a sketch of how the wires are connected. If they're spliced with wirenuts, unscrew them and untwist the wires. If the wires are spliced only with electrician's tape, simply unwind the tape. New splices will be covered with wirenuts. Lay the old fixture aside.

As your helper holds up the new fixture, match its wires to the old wires as shown in your sketch. Splice with wirenuts (see page 96).

Secure the new fixture by reversing the steps you took to loosen the original, using any new hardware included with the fixture. If you need to patch the wall or ceiling, see page 110.

Adding new fixtures. Installing a new surface-mounted fixture is much like replacing one, once the cable has been routed from a power source and the fixture box and switch installed.

New nonmetallic cable routed to the box should include a grounding wire, which is attached to the box's grounding screw. If more than one cable enters the box (for example, a separate cable may be connected to the switch box), you'll need to attach the end of a short length of #12 wire (a "jumper") to the ground-

ing screw and splice its other end to the ends of the grounding wires in the cables. Cap the splice with a wirenut.

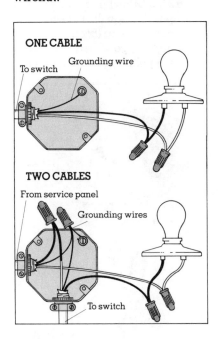

ONE CABLE

To switch
Grounding wire

TWO CABLES

From service panel
Grounding wires
To switch

A cord or chain-hung fixture must also have a grounding wire run from the socket to the box (see page 98).

Match the box's wires to those of the new fixture—black wire to black, white to white, as shown at left. Cap all splices with wirenuts. Then mount the fixture with the hardware specified by the manufacturer.

Installing track systems

Track systems are mounted, either directly or with mounting clips, to the wall or ceiling. Power is provided from a fixture box or through a cord plugged into an existing outlet. Tracks are often wired into two separate circuits controlled by two switches. For greater flexibility of light level and placement, install one switch plus a dimmer switch (see page 101).

Connecting the system. A plug-in connector, which includes a 12-foot cord and a lamp plug, lets you place a track wherever the cord will reach an outlet. Plug-in connectors are available only with single-circuit tracks.

A track system with a wire-in connector is hooked up directly to a fixture box. You may be able to use an existing box, or you may have to install a new one (see pages 94–95). In either case, you'll need as many wall switches as your track has circuits. If you're simply replacing a fixture with a single-circuit track system, you can use the wall switch already wired to the old fixture, or replace that switch with a dimmer.

Mounting the track. Once the power is tapped and the proper switches are installed, it's time to attach the track connector to the ceiling, wall, or fixture box (see drawing above).

(Continued on next page)

... Light fixtures

For attaching a track or mounting clips to the ceiling or wall, you'll use screws or toggle bolts in predrilled holes. To lay out and drill the necessary holes, line up a chalkline or the edge of a yardstick with the center slot of the connector; snap or draw a line to the proposed end of the track.

Setting a length of track beside the line, mark along the line the positions of the knockout holes in the roof of the track. These marks show you where to drill.

Because a plug-in connector lies flush against the wall or ceiling surface, you can attach the track directly to the surface. Slip the two bare wire ends of the first length of track into the connector receptacles; secure the track with screws or toggle bolts. Proceed in a similar manner with the remaining lengths of track.

A wire-in connector holds the ends of the track ¼ to ½ inch away from the mounting surface. You'll need special clips to hold the track at the same level. Once clips are screwed or bolted to the ceiling or wall, slip the first length of track into the connector; press it, and succeeding lengths, into the clips.

Installing recessed fixtures

Common recessed fixtures include incandescent circular or square downlights and larger fluorescent ceiling or "troffer" panels. You'll need to cut a hole in the ceiling between the joists, or remove tiles or panels from a suspended ceiling, to install either type. Larger fixtures may also require 2 by 4 blocking between joists for support.

Recessed fixtures need several inches of clearance above the finished ceiling. They're most easily installed below an unfinished attic or crawlspace. Because of the heat generated by many downlights, you must allow adequate air flow around the fixture; remove insulation within 3 inches of the fixture and make sure that no combustible materials are within ½ inch (with the exception of any joists or other blocking used for support).

Recessed downlights. Recessed downlights fall into two types: one comes prewired and grounded to its housing box; the other must be wired into a junction box previously nailed to a joist. Larger downlights may require the same type of support blocking described below for ceiling panels.

Before installing the downlight, you'll need to cut a hole for the fixture housing in the ceiling between two joists; in a suspended ceiling, simply remove one tile or panel.

Once you've determined the proper location, trace the outline of the fixture housing on the ceiling with a pencil; use a keyhole saw or saber saw to neatly cut the hole.

• **Downlight with box.** This type of fixture and its box are premounted on a metal frame (see drawing below). The unit is (A) first slipped through the hole cut in the ceiling and then (B) clipped to the ceiling's edge. Then the fixture housing (C) snaps into its socket.

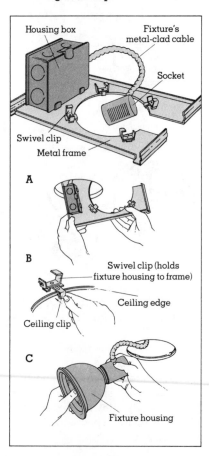

Housing box

Fixture's metal-clad cable

Socket

Swivel clip

Metal frame

A

B

Swivel clip (holds fixture housing to frame)

Ceiling edge

Ceiling clip

C

Fixture housing

• **Downlight without box.** To link this type of fixture with incoming cable, it's important to first select a junction box that can be nailed to a joist, as shown below. The fixture's metal-clad ("flex") cable is clamped and wired into the junction box. The fixture housing snaps into its socket, then the fixture is pushed into place and secured with clips to the ceiling material. The metal-clad cable grounds the fixture to the box.

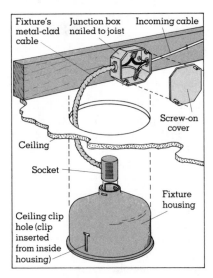

Fixture's metal-clad cable

Junction box nailed to joist

Incoming cable

Screw-on cover

Ceiling

Socket

Fixture housing

Ceiling clip hole (clip inserted from inside housing)

Recessed ceiling panels. Manufactured ceiling panels, or troffer units, are available in a range of sizes. Panels are often designed to fit exactly the space of a panel or tile in a suspended ceiling (see page 107). The fixture rests on the furring strips or metal channel that support the ceiling panels.

In a standard ceiling, you'll have to cut a hole between joists, build a support frame, and fasten the fixture to the frame. If you don't have access from the attic or crawlspace above, you may need to cut an oversize opening in the ceiling in order to install the support framing; you'll have to patch the ceiling later.

To prepare for the fixture, first mark its outline on the ceiling between two joists. (See page 85 for help in locating joists). Then, with a keyhole or saber saw, cut through the ceiling along the line and remove the material. Cut lengths of 2 by 4 scrap to fit snugly between adjacent joists. Nail the 2 by 4s flush with the bottoms of the joists, spaced to match the width or length of your fixture. Use extra blocking parallel to the joists as needed (see drawing below).

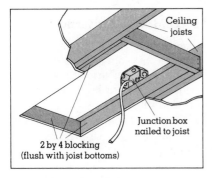

Ceiling joists

Junction box nailed to joist

2 by 4 blocking (flush with joist bottoms)

If your panel is wider than the space between adjacent joists, you'll need to cut away a portion of one joist and install headers to reinforce the gap. See "Skylight basics," page 89, for more details.

To provide electrical power, route cable to the ceiling panel from a junction box, switch box, or adjacent fixture box. The panel often has its own cover plate, or "box," to protect wire splices; if yours doesn't, nail a junction box nearby to house the connections.

If your only access is from below, connect the wiring to the panel before pushing the panel into the opening. Anchor the panel to the blocking or joists with nails, screws, or mounting hardware provided by the manufacturer.

Installing dimmer switches

Most dimmer switches can be wired into existing circuits in the same way as the switches they replace. (See page 96 for details on wiring switches.) The one exception is a dimmer for a fluorescent fixture, which requires some added steps and hardware.

Incandescent dimmers. Usually a single switch controls a light or a group of lights. This type of switch is called a single-pole switch; it must be replaced with a single-pole dimmer.

Sometimes two switches control a light or group of lights, as at opposite ends of the kitchen. These are called three-way switches. If you want to add a dimmer to such a system, replace the three-way switch most frequently used with a three-way dimmer. Leave the second three-way switch in place.

Before installing a dimmer, make sure the power to the switch box is turned OFF. After you've unscrewed the switch plate and switch-mounting screws, pull the switch from its box. Detach the wires from the terminals on the switch and reattach them to similar terminals on the dimmer.

If the dimmer comes with short wires instead of terminals, use wirenuts to splice their free ends to the wires in the switch box. A typical three-way dimmer is shown below (for details on using wirenuts, see page 96).

On three-way switches and dimmers, one of the terminals will be marked "common"; the wire attached to the common terminal on the switch is attached to the common terminal on the dimmer.

Fluorescent dimmers. If you're considering a dimmer for a fluorescent fixture, first make sure the fixture is equipped with rapid-start tubes; modern dimmers won't function with old-style preheat tubes. Then you must replace the ballast (transformer) in the fixture with a special dimming ballast. A typical wiring situation is shown below.

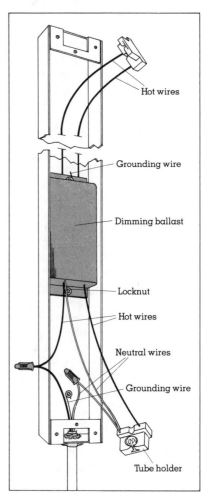

Hot wires

Grounding wire

Dimming ballast

Locknut

Hot wires

Neutral wires

Grounding wire

Tube holder

Use a dimming ballast with two hot wires and matching dimmer to avoid rewiring the run between them with five-wire cable—a difficult chore. Wire the two-wire fluorescent dimmer into the switch box as you would an incandescent dimmer.

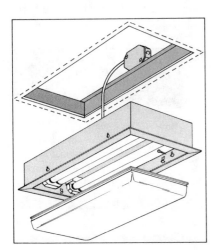

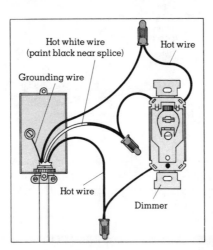

Hot white wire (paint black near splice)

Hot wire

Grounding wire

Hot wire

Dimmer

UNDER-CABINET LIGHTING—A TASK FORCE

The constant demand for additional kitchen storage pays an unexpected dividend to homeowners searching for ways to light work centers. Make your cabinets and shelves do double duty: attach task lights underneath them to shed bright, even light over the sink, range, menu-planning center, or other areas requiring supplemental illumination.

Many types of incandescent and fluorescent fixtures—ready-made or for you to assemble—are available for installation beneath cabinets and shelves.

Fluorescent fixtures

A popular choice for task lighting, fluorescent fixtures spread a diffuse light that minimizes shadows. Their long, slender shapes and low operating temperatures make them ideal choices for under-cabinet installation. Fluorescent tubes are also twice as efficient as incandescent bulbs and last from five to ten times as long.

Fluorescent lights can be permanently wired into electric circuitry or plugged into nearby outlets. If each fixture is operated from its own switch, you'll have greatest control of the light and least waste of energy. Dimmers may be added to lower the intensity at times when only general illumination is required.

One of the most common types of fluorescent lighting, and one of the easiest to install, is an integral unit composed of one or two tubes and a ballast. For greatest efficiency, the fixture should span at least two-thirds of the area to be lighted and should be positioned as close as possible to the front of the cabinet.

Adding a wood or metal valance to a fixture mounted at eye level hides the unit and eliminates glare (see illustration below).

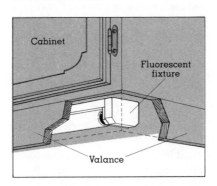

To build a valance to match your cabinet's decor, measure the required space and cut a piece of cardboard to use as a mockup.

For more flexibility, you can buy lengths of metal strip lights and join them to extend the light under a cabinet of any size. The strips are equipped with built-in valances in a choice of finishes. Besides accommodating fluorescent bulbs, the systems offer incandescent spotlight (see illustration below) and mini-light options.

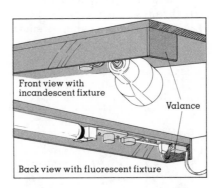

Front view with incandescent fixture

Valance

Back view with fluorescent fixture

To install strips under wooden cabinets or shelves, simply screw them into the lower surface. Mounting clips easily attach a unit to glass shelves.

Incandescent alternatives

Incandescent task-lighting options include curio lights (similar to those mounted on picture frames), strip lighting to buy or build, and miniature track lights.

Incandescent bulbs can be plugged into the strip lighting unit mentioned above, or you can assemble your own components (see below). The two most common types of strips are plug-ins, with bulbs positioned in set locations, and parallel conductor strips, in which bulbs can be positioned all along the length of the strip.

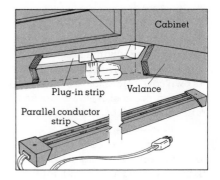

Cabinet

Plug-in strip   Valance

Parallel conductor strip

Miniature track lights (see illustration below) work just like their larger relatives. Installation is similar to that for strip lighting. Continuous electrical tracks allow you to position fixtures where you choose.

Miniature track lights

Walls & ceilings

Installing a new wall (see page 84) or a suspended ceiling can change the entire appearance of your room. Or you can give your kitchen a completely new look simply by splashing on a coat of colorful paint or by applying a complementary wall covering.

Even adding a new wall surface is relatively easy. Gypsum wallboard, the most popular choice, is inexpensive and provides a good surface for paint, wallpaper, tile, plastic laminate, or paneling.

Fortunately, these improvements are among the easiest projects for the average homeowner to tackle—many of the new products on the market require little or no experience to apply.

If your kitchen's ceiling is something you'd like to hide, a lightweight, trim solution might be to install a suspended ceiling with metal grid frame and fiberboard panels. Such a ceiling also permits easy installation of recessed light fixtures for both general and task lighting (see pages 100–101).

Installing gypsum wallboard

Cutting and installing gypsum wallboard is a straightforward procedure, but concealing the joints between panels and in the corners demands patience and care. And the weight of full panels can be awkward to negotiate. Wallboard is easily damaged; take care not to bend or break the corners or tear the paper covers.

Standard wallboard panels are 4 feet wide and from 8 feet to 16 feet long. Common thicknesses are ⅜ inch for a backing material for other wall coverings, ½ inch for final wall coverings, and ⅝ inch where the walls border a garage space. Choose water-resistant wallboard, identified by green or blue paper covers, in the sink area or wherever moisture might collect.

Cutting wallboard. To make a straight cut, first mark the cut line on the front paper layer with a pencil and straightedge, or snap a line with a chalkline. Cut through the front paper with a utility knife.

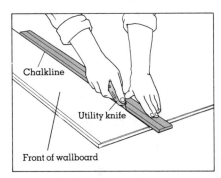

Turn the wallboard over and break the gypsum core by bending it toward the back. Finally, cut the back paper along the bend. Smooth the edge of the cut with a perforated rasp.

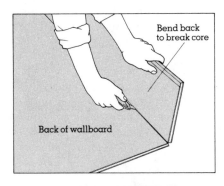

When fitting wallboard around obstructions such as doorways or electrical outlet boxes, carefully measure from the edge of an adjacent wallboard panel or reference point to the obstruction. Transfer the measurements to a new panel, and cut out the correct area. For openings within a panel, drill a pilot hole and make the cutout with a keyhole or wallboard saw. Larger edge cutouts should also be made with a keyhole or wallboard saw.

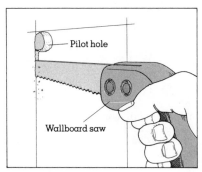

Nailing the panels. Before installing panels, mark the stud locations on the floor and ceiling. Center the wallboard edges over two studs and fasten with wallboard nails. Drive in the nails with a hammer, dimpling the wallboard surface without puncturing the paper. Nail the panel to the inside studs. Nail spacing will be specified by local codes. Typical spacing is every 6 inches.

If your wallboard will serve as a backing for ceramic tile, paneling, or cabinets, you may not need to hide joints and corners. But if

HOW TO INSTALL GYPSUM WALLBOARD

Lift the wallboard panel into position (A) and center the edges over wall studs. Then nail the panel to the studs (B), dimpling the wallboard surface slightly with the hammer.

... Walls & ceilings

HOW TO TAPE WALLBOARD JOINTS

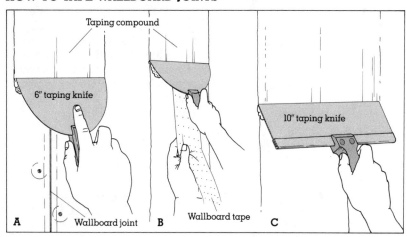

Taping compound

6" taping knife

10" taping knife

A   Wallboard joint   B   Wallboard tape   C

To tape a wallboard joint, spread a smooth layer of taping compound over the joint (A), embed paper tape in compound (B), and apply a second, thinner layer of compound. When it's dry, sand smooth and apply a wider layer (C), feathering the edges.

you're painting or wallpapering, you'll want to finish the wallboard.

Taping joints and corners. To finish wallboard neatly, you'll need wallboard tape (buy tape that's precreased) and taping compound.

The taping process is done in stages. To tape a joint between panels, first apply a smooth layer of taping compound over the joint with a 6-inch taping knife. Before the compound dries, embed wallboard tape into it and apply another thin coat of compound over the tape, smoothing it gently with the knife.

To tape an inside corner, apply a smooth layer of compound to the wallboard on each side of the corner. Measure and tear the tape, fold it in half vertically along the crease, and press it into the corner with a corner tool. Apply a thin layer of compound over the tape and smooth it out with the corner tool.

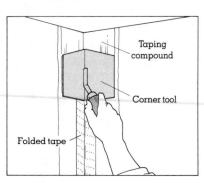

Taping compound

Corner tool

Folded tape

Exterior corners are covered with a protective metal cornerbead and finished with compound.

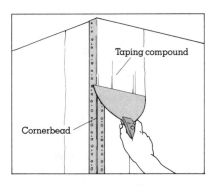

Taping compound

Cornerbead

Continue taping all the joints. Then, using smooth, even strokes with the 6-inch knife, cover the inside nail dimples with compound.

Allow the taping compound to dry for at least 24 hours before sanding lightly to get a smooth surface. (NOTE: Wear a face mask and goggles while sanding.

Using a 10-inch knife, apply a second coat of compound, feathering out the edges past each side of the taped joint.

Let the second coat dry. Then sand it and apply a final coat. Use a 10-inch or an even wider knife to smooth out and feather the edges, covering all dimples and joints. After the compound dries, sand it again to remove even minor imperfections.

Painting your kitchen

A fresh coat of paint provides the fastest way to "remodel" your kitchen. Below are some guidelines to help you do a good job.

Choosing the paint. Your basic choices in paint are latex (water-base) paint (also called acrylic or vinyl) and oil-base paint. For help with your decision, see page 44.

Tools of the trade. Choosing the correct brushes is almost as important as selecting the paint.

- **Natural bristles** (hog hairs) are traditionally used to apply oil-base paints. They should not be used with latex paint; the bristles soak up water from the paint and quickly become soggy and useless.

- **Synthetic bristles,** nylon or nylon-like, are best for applying latex, but most can also be used with oil-base paints.

What size brush do you need? For window sashes, shutters, and trim, choose a 1½ or 2-inch angled sash brush. For woodwork and other medium-size surfaces, a 2 or 3-inch brush is best. And for walls, ceilings, and most paneling, choose a 3½ or 4-inch brush—if brushing is your choice.

When you want to paint a large flat area quickly and easily, though, a roller is the answer. A 9-inch roller will handle all interior paint jobs. A handle threaded to accommodate an extension pole will allow you to reach high walls and ceilings without a ladder or scaffolding. The roller's cover, like paint brush bristles, is important—choose a nylon blend for latex, lambskin for oil-base paint, or a mohair cover for use with both. A well-designed roller tray is also essential.

A pad applicator, which resembles a sponge attached to a short handle, is handy for clean edging and for use in tight spots.

Preparing the surface. A key factor in preventing cracking and peeling after the paint dries is preparing the

TOOLS OF THE PAINTING TRADE

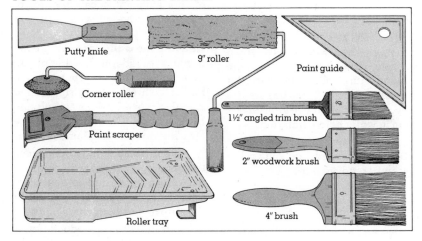

Putty knife

9" roller

Paint guide

Corner roller

Paint scraper

1½" angled trim brush

2" woodwork brush

4" brush

Roller tray

surface correctly. It's *essential* to the bonding and durability of any latex paint application.

Start by removing light fixtures and faceplates. Then inspect the area you're painting for small holes as well as more extensive damage, and make all necessary repairs.

If an old paint finish is flaking, you must sand it smooth. And when you paint over a glossy surface, you must first roughen the old finish with sandpaper so the new paint will adhere. Use a sponge soaked with paint thinner on any spots that are very greasy. Then an overall dusting, a sponging with an abrasive cleanser, and rinsing (complete a small area at a time) will finish off the surface preparation. Allow about 24 hours for all washed areas to dry completely.

Sometimes an old finish is in such poor condition that the paint must be removed entirely. The easiest method of stripping old paint is to apply a commercial liquid paint remover, then scrape off the softened paint with a broad knife or paint scraper. Finish the surface by sanding lightly until it's clean and smooth.

It's possible to paint over wallpaper that's smooth and attached firmly to the wall. Apply a sealing primer such as pigmented shellac or a flat oil-base enamel undercoat. Let the sealer dry completely before you paint.

It's often safer, though, to re-move the wallpaper, especially if it's tearing and flaking. See "Hanging new wallpaper" for details.

Unpainted plaster or wallboard should be primed with latex paint or latex primer-sealer. Prime unpainted wood with oil-base paint whether you plan to finish with oil-base or latex.

Painting tips. If you're painting both walls and ceiling, start with the ceiling. Paint the entire ceiling without stopping. You'll want to paint in rectangles, approximately 2 feet by 3 feet, starting in a corner and working across the ceiling in the direction of the shortest distance.

Begin the first section by using a brush, pad applicator, or special corner roller to paint a narrow strip next to the wall line and around any fixtures. Then finish the section with a roller, overlapping any brush marks. Continue painting, one section at a time, from one end of the ceiling to the other and back again.

Then it's on to the walls. Mentally divide a wall into 3-foot-square sections, starting from a corner at the ceiling line and working down the wall. As with ceilings, use a brush, pad applicator, or corner roller along the ceiling line, corners, fixtures, or edges of openings. Finish each section with a roller, overlapping any brush marks.

At the bottom edge along the floor, or baseboard, or along the edges of cabinets and counters, use

a brush and paint guide; as before, overlap the brush strokes with a roller. Return to the ceiling line and again work down in 3-foot sections.

Hanging new wallpaper

Next to paint, wallpaper is the most popular covering for kitchen walls. Easier than ever to install, wallpaper is available in a kaleidoscope of colors and patterns.

Choices for the kitchen. A wallpaper for the kitchen should be scrubbable, durable, and stain resistant. *Solid vinyl* wallpapers, available in a wide variety of colors and textures, fill the bill. *Vinyl coatings* also give wallpaper a washable surface but aren't notably durable or grease resistant.

If you're a beginner, you may want to consider prepasted and pre-trimmed paper.

To find an adhesive suitable for your material, check the manufacturer's instructions or ask your dealer.

Preparing the surface. To prepare for papering, you'll need to remove all light fixtures and faceplates. Thoroughly clean and rinse the surface. Most manufacturers recommend that you completely remove any old wallpaper before hanging a nonporous covering like solid vinyl.

If the existing paper is strippable, it will come off easily when you pull it up at a corner or seam. To remove nonstrippable wallpaper, use either a steamer (available for rent from your dealer) or a spray bottle filled with very hot water. Before steaming, break the surface of the old paper by sanding it with very coarse sandpaper or by pulling a sawblade sideways across the wall.

Within a few minutes of steaming (wait longer if it's a nonporous material), you can begin to remove the old paper. Using a broad knife, work down from the top of the wall, scraping off the old wallpaper.

If yours is a new gypsum wallboard surface, tape all joints between panels (see page 104) before papering. When dry, sand the wall

... Walls & ceilings

smooth and apply a coat of flat, oil-base primer-sealer.

If you want to apply wallpaper over previously painted surfaces that are in good condition, simply clean off all the dirt, grease, and oil, and let it dry. If latex paint was used, or if you can't determine the type, you must apply an oil-base undercoat over the old paint.

Ready to start? Plan the best place to hang your first strip. If you're papering all four walls with a patterned paper, the last strip you hang probably won't match the first, so plan to start and finish in the least conspicuous place—usually a corner, door casing, or window casing.

Most house walls are not straight and plumb, so you'll need to establish a plumb line. Figure the width of your first strip of wallpaper minus ½ inch (which will overlap the corner or casing); measure that distance from your starting point, and mark the wall. Using a carpenter's level as a straightedge, draw a line through your mark that's perfectly plumb. Extend the line until it reaches from floor to ceiling.

It's a good idea to measure the wall height before cutting each strip of wallpaper. Allow 2 inches extra at the top and bottom. Be sure also to allow for pattern match.

Using a razor knife, cut the strips. Number them on the back at the top edge so you can apply them in the proper sequence.

With some wallpapers, you'll need to spread adhesive on the backing with a wide, soft paint roller or pasting brush; other papers are prepasted—all you have to do is soak them in water before hanging.

After pasting or soaking, strips should be "booked," as shown below, until ready to hang.

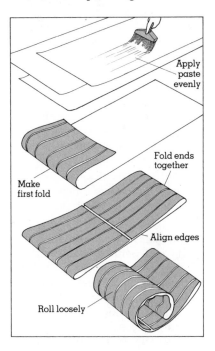

Apply paste evenly

Make first fold

Fold ends together

Align edges

Roll loosely

Trim the edges of the wallpaper at this stage, if necessary. You're now ready to hang the paper.

Hanging the wallpaper. First, position a stepladder next to the plumb line you've marked. Open the top fold of the first booked strip, raising it so that it overlaps the ceiling line by 2 inches. Carefully align the strip's edge with the plumb line.

Using a smoothing brush, press the strip against the wall. Smooth out all wrinkles and air bubbles. Then release the lower portion of the strip and smooth it into place.

Carefully roll the edges flat, if necessary, with a seam roller. To trim along the ceiling and baseboard, use a broad knife and a very sharp razor knife. With a sponge dipped in lukewarm water, remove any excess adhesive before it dries.

Unfold your second strip on the wall in the same way you did the first. Gently butt the second strip against the first, aligning the pattern as you move down the wall. Continue around the room with the remaining paper.

Dealing with corners. Because few rooms have perfectly straight corners, you'll have to measure from the edge of the preceding strip to the corner; do this at three heights.

HANGING THE FIRST STRIP

2" overlap
Plumb line
A

½" overlap
B

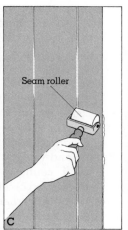
Seam roller
C

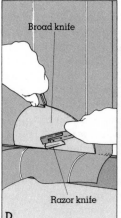
Broad knife
Razor knife
D

Sponge
E

To hang wallpaper, first open the top fold of the strip, overlap the ceiling line, and align the strip's edge with the plumb line (A); press the strip against the wall with a smoothing brush (B). Release the lower fold and smooth into place; roll the edges flat with a seam roller (C). Trim the strip along the ceiling and baseboard with a broad knife and a razor knife (D). Remove excess adhesive with a sponge dipped in lukewarm water (E).

Cut a strip ½ inch wider than the widest measurement. Butting the strip to the preceding strip, brush it firmly into and around the corner. At the top and bottom corners, cut the overlap so the strip will lie flat.

Next, measure the width of the leftover piece of wallpaper. On the adjacent wall, measure the same distance from the corner and make a plumb line at that point.

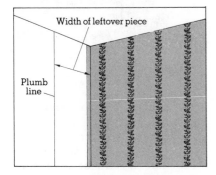

Position one edge of the strip along the plumb line; the other edge will cover the ½-inch overlap. (If you're hanging vinyl wallpaper, you should apply a vinyl-to-vinyl adhesive on top of the overlap.)

Cutouts. It's easy to cut around electrical switches and plug-in outlets. Be sure all faceplates have been removed before hanging the wallpaper; then before making the cutout, shut off the electricity.

Hang the paper as described above. Then use a razor knife to make an X-shaped cut over the opening, extending the cuts to each corner. Trim the excess along the edges of the opening with the razor knife and a broad knife.

Installing a suspended ceiling

Easy-to-install suspended ceilings consist of a metal grid suspended from above with wire or spring-type hangers. The grid holds acoustic or decorative fiberboard panels.

The most common panel size is 2 feet by 4 feet, though panels are available in a variety of sizes. Transparent and translucent panels and egg-crate grilles are made to fit the gridwork to admit light from

HOW TO INSTALL A SUSPENDED CEILING

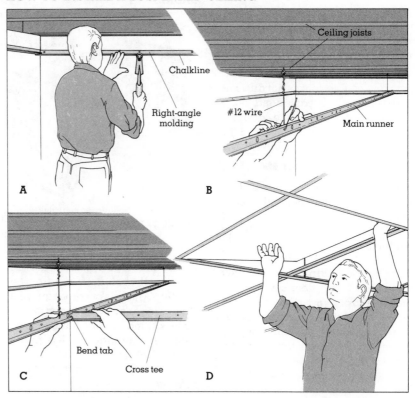

To hang a suspended ceiling, snap a chalkline around the room and install L-shaped molding with its base on the chalkline (A). Set the main runners on the molding at each end, attach them to the joists with #12 wire (B), lock 4-foot cross tees to the main runners (C), and push the panels into place (D).

above. Recessed lighting panels that exactly replace one panel also are available from some manufacturers. All components are replaceable, and the panels can be raised for access to the area above.

Figuring your needs. Here is the easiest way to determine the number of panels you'll need: Measure your wall lengths at the proposed ceiling height. Draw the ceiling area to scale on graph paper, using one square per foot of ceiling size. Block in the panel size you'll be using. Finally, count the blocked areas and parts of areas to get the number of panels you'll need.

For a professional-looking job, plan equal borders on the opposite sides of the room. To determine the nonstandard width of panels needed for perimeter rows, measure the extra space from the last full row of panels to one wall and divide by two. This final figure will be the

dimension of border tiles against that wall and the opposite wall. Repeat this procedure for the other room dimensions.

Installing the ceiling. First, figure the ceiling height—at least 3 inches below plumbing, 5 inches below lights (minimum ceiling height is 7 feet 6 inches). Snap a chalkline around the room at that level and install L-shaped angle molding with its base on the chalkline.

Next, install the main runners perpendicular to the ceiling joists, (see above). Cut the runners to length with tinsnips. Setting them on the molding at each end, support them every 4 feet with #12 wire attached to small eyebolts screwed into joists above. Lock 4-foot cross tees to the main runners by bending the tabs in the runner spots.

Set the panels into place and install any recessed lighting panels. Cut border panels as necessary.

Cabinets & countertops

Installing new cabinets and dressing them up with the countertops of your choice can be the passport to a whole new world of kitchen style and efficiency.

Removing and installing cabinets and countertops is not difficult and requires only basic hand tools. But the work must be done carefully to ensure a professional-looking fit.

Removing old cabinets

If you remove base cabinets first, you'll have room to get underneath wall cabinets without strain, and you'll avoid damaging walls or cabinets.

Base cabinets. First, pry away any vinyl wall base, floor covering, or molding from the base cabinet's kickspace or sides, as shown above. Next, disconnect plumbing supply lines and the drain trap from the kitchen sink (see page 121). Also disconnect plumbing and electrical lines to a dishwasher or garbage disposer (see page 122), electric or gas range, wall ovens, or cooktop (see pages 125–126). *Be sure plumbing and gas lines and electrical circuits are properly shut off before disconnecting them.* Remove the sink, fixtures, and appliances from the area.

Old base cabinets are usually attached to wall studs with screws or nails through nailing strips at the back of each unit. Sometimes they're also fastened to the floor with nails through the kickspace trim or cabinet sides. Screws are easy to remove unless they're old and stripped. To remove nails, you may need to pry the cabinet away from the wall or floor with a pry bar (use a wood scrap between the pry bar and the wall or floor to prevent damaging those surfaces).

Several base units may be fastened together and covered with a single countertop. If you can remove the entire assembly intact, you'll save time and labor. Otherwise, unscrew or pry the units apart—they're fastened either through adjacent sides or face frames—and remove the countertop.

CABINET ANATOMY

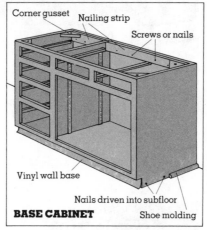

BASE CABINET

Labels: Corner gusset, Nailing strip, Screws or nails, Vinyl wall base, Nails driven into subfloor, Shoe molding

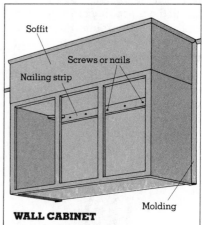

WALL CABINET

Labels: Soffit, Screws or nails, Nailing strip, Molding

Countertops typically are anchored to the cabinet frame from below, through rails or corner gussets. Plastic laminate, hardwood butcherblock, and the backing for ceramic tile countertops are normally fastened with screws; masonry and synthetic marble are attached with adhesive.

Wall cabinets. Once the base cabinets are out of the way, you're ready to remove the wall cabinets. They're either screwed, bolted, or nailed through nailing strips at the back of the cabinets to wall studs behind each unit. They might also be fastened to the ceiling or an overhead soffit.

If the cabinets are screwed or bolted to the wall, recruit some helpers to hold them in place while you unfasten them. Then remove the cabinets from the area. If the cabinets are fastened with nails, you'll have to use a pry bar. Again, individual units are probably fastened together. If you have a helper or two, the assembly can often be removed intact.

Installing new cabinets

Both wall and base cabinets are carefully aligned with layout marks previously drawn on the walls. Then they're fastened to the wall studs with screws. In order to give yourself adequate working room, and prevent damage to base cabinets, it's best to install wall cabinets first.

Wall cabinets. Your first task is to locate and mark wall studs in the area of your new cabinets. (For help in finding studs, see page 85.) Snap a chalkline to mark the studs' centers, or draw lines with a soft pencil.

Next you'll need to lay out lines on the wall for the top and bottom of the cabinets. Measure up 84 inches from the floor (the standard top height for wall cabinets). Because floors are seldom completely level, measure in several spots and use the highest mark as your reference point. Trace a line from this mark across the wall, using a carpenter's level as a straightedge.

Now subtract the exact height of the new cabinet units from the top line, and draw this line on the wall. Tack a temporary ledger strip made from 1 by 2 or 2 by 4 lumber to the wall studs, with the ledger's top edge exactly flush with the bottom line.

Start your cabinet installation either from a corner of the kitchen or from the edge of the first cabinet. You can determine the location of the latter from your kitchen plans. Again, mark the wall.

Remove cabinet doors by their hinge pins, if possible. Then, with as much help as you can recruit, lift the first cabinet into place atop the ledger strip. While your helpers hold the cabinet in position, drill pilot holes through the top and bottom nailing strips and into wall studs; *loosely* fasten the cabinet to the studs with woodscrews long enough to

HOW TO MARK REFERENCE LINES

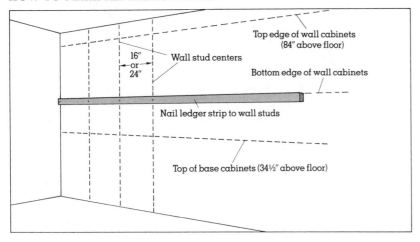

Top edge of wall cabinets (84″ above floor)

16″ or 24″

Wall stud centers

Bottom edge of wall cabinets

Nail ledger strip to wall studs

Top of base cabinets (34½″ above floor)

extend 1½ inches into the studs when tight.

At this point, some careful attention to detail will ensure a first-rate installation. Check the cabinet carefully for level and plumb—from top to bottom and from front to back—with your carpenter's level. Because walls seldom are exactly plumb, you may have to make some fine adjustments to enable the cabinet to hang correctly. Bumps and high points on the wall can sometimes be sanded down; low points will need to be shimmed.

Drive shims as needed between the cabinet back and the wall, either down from the top or up from the bottom (in which case you'll need to remove the ledger strip). Tap the shims in a little at a time, and keep checking with the level. When all is in order, tighten the woodscrews; then recheck with the level. If the tightening has thrown the cabinet out of plumb, shim again.

Some cabinets are designed with "scribing strips" along the sides—extra material you can shave down to achieve a perfect fit between the cabinet and an irregular wall. To scribe a cabinet, first position it; then run a length of masking tape down the side to be scribed. Setting the points of a compass with pencil to the widest gap between the scribing strip and the wall, run the compass pivot down the wall next to the strip, as shown above right. The wall's irregularities will

be marked on the tape. Remove the cabinet from the wall, and use a block plane, file, or power belt sander to trim the scribing strip to the line. Then reinstall the cabinet.

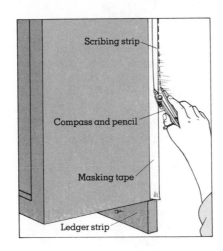

Scribing strip

Compass and pencil

Masking tape

Ledger strip

If your cabinets don't have scribing strips, you can cover any large irregularities with decorative molding or latex caulk.

Adjacent wall cabinets may be joined together on the wall or on the floor; clamp them together with C-clamps, carefully align the front edges, and screw together adjacent cabinet sides or face frames, as shown at right.

Base cabinets. Though base cabinets are less awkward to position than wall cabinets, you must now deal with the vagaries of both wall and floor.

Before you begin, remove any baseboard, moldings, or wall base that might interfere. From the floor, measure up 34½ inches—the height of a standard base cabinet.

Again, take several measurements and use the highest mark for your reference point. Draw a level line through the mark and across the wall.

If you need to cut access holes in a cabinet's back or bottom for plumbing supply and drain pipes, or for electrical wire serving the sink complex, you'll want to do so *before* you install the cabinet.

With helpers, move the cabinet into position, threading any plumbing connections or wiring through the access holes. Measure the cabinet carefully for level and plumb—from side to side and front to back. Then shim the unit as necessary between the cabinet base and floor.

Scribing strips may be included along the sides to allow full alignment with the wall. Both shims and irregularities in the floor can be hidden by baseboard trim, vinyl wall base, or new flooring.

When the cabinet is aligned, drill pilot holes through the nailing strip at the back of the cabinet into the wall studs. Fasten the unit to the studs with woodscrews.

Once installed, base cabinets are fastened together like wall cabinets: screw together the adjacent sides or face frames. Now it's time to install the new countertop; for instructions, see pages 111–113.

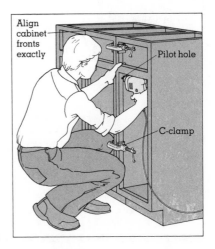

Align cabinet fronts exactly

Pilot hole

C-clamp

TIPS FOR PATCHING WALLBOARD & PLASTER

Sometimes, all it takes to add new life to kitchen walls are a few repairs and a fresh coat of paint. Gypsum wallboard and plaster, the two most common wall materials, are not difficult to patch, but you'll have to work carefully to match the patch to the surrounding surface.

Patching gypsum wallboard

Cracks, nail holes, or gouge marks can be patched with a putty knife and either spackling compound or patching plaster; cracks may also be filled with a special crack patcher.

To patch holes between wall studs, first cut a neat rectangle around the hole with a sharp utility knife or hacksaw blade. Then, from another piece of wallboard, cut a rectangle 1 inch larger on all sides. Laying the new piece face side down, recut it the same size as the wall rectangle—*without* scoring the paper on the face side. Lift off the inch of cut board around all sides, leaving the paper margins intact (A).

Spread a thin layer of spackling compound around and on the edges of the hole. Position the patch (B) and cover the seams and entire surface with a thin coating of spackle. Let it dry; then smooth carefully with fine sandpaper.

Large holes will normally uncover at least one wall stud, which may be used as a nailing surface for the new patch. Or you can enlarge the hole to use two flanking studs as nailing surfaces. For best support, nail the patch to horizontal blocking installed between the studs. Install, and finish the patch as if you were installing a brand new panel (see pages 103-104 for techniques).

Patching plaster walls

Small cracks in plaster are treated exactly like those in wallboard, except that extra steps may be required to match the present surface texture (see below).

For holes or wide cracks that go all the way to the lath or wallboard backing, first knock out all loose, cracked plaster with a hammer and chisel. Undercut the edges to strengthen the eventual bond. Using a sponge, dampen the area surrounding the hole.

If the hole is larger than 4 inches square, it will take three layers to fill. The first layer should fill a little more than half the depth and should bond to the lath backing (A). Before this layer dries (about 4 hours), score it with a nail (B) to provide a "bite" for succeeding layers.

Re-wet the dried patch and apply a second layer. This coat should come within ½ inch to ¼ inch of the surface. Again, let the patching plaster dry; then apply the third coat.

To fill deep holes without backing (for example, where an electrical housing box has been removed), first pry out any cracked material around the hole and dust the area thoroughly. Then loop a length of wire through a piece of rust-resistant screen, as shown below. Push the screen through the hole to be filled, and wind it tightly back against the wall with the wire and a stick (A). Wet the wall adjacent to the hole, and fill the hole with patching plaster to half its depth (B). When the patch is dry, cut off the wire and finish filling the hole.

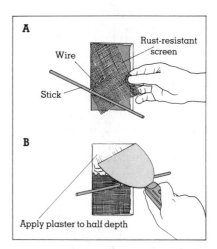

Apply plaster to half depth

Matching an existing texture requires special treatment of the still-wet plaster. For a smooth surface, pull a wide putty knife or a rubber float across the surface; to achieve an almost glossy smoothness, wipe the plaster with a wet sponge held in one hand, just ahead of the float in the other hand. For a rough surface, scour lightly with a paint brush—either in swirling strokes or jabbed straight at the wall, depending on the texture you're matching.

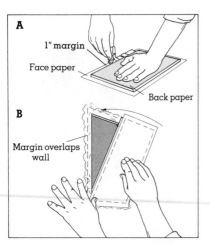

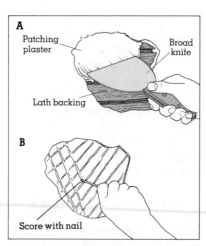

.. Cabinets & countertops

Installing plastic laminate countertops

Plastic laminate countertops, by far the most common countertops used in kitchens, are divided into two types: post-formed and self-rimmed (for self-rimmed, see page 112).

Post-formed countertops are premolded one-piece tops, from curved backsplash to bullnosed front. They're available in several standard lengths (usually from 6 to 12 feet) and can be cut to the exact length you need. Most types are offered with accessory kits for endsplashes (where the countertop meets a side wall or cabinet) and endcaps.

The term "self-rimmed" simply means that you apply the laminate of your choice over an old countertop or new core material. Though post-formed countertops are simpler to install, building your own enables you to choose from a much greater selection of laminates. You can also tailor the dimensions of the backsplash, endsplash, and overhang to your exact requirements.

Post-formed countertop. Since post-formed countertops come only in standard sizes, you'll normally need to buy one slightly larger than you need and cut it to length. To cut the countertop with a handsaw, mark the cut line on the face. Mark the back if you're using a power saw. Use masking tape to protect the cutting line against chipping (you'll probably have to draw the line again, this time on the tape). Smooth the edge of the cut with a file or sandpaper. Plan to cover that end with an endcap or endsplash.

Exactly what size do you need? The standard overhang on a laminate top varies between ¾ inch and 1 inch in front and on open ends. Add these dimensions to the dimensions of your cabinet. If you plan to include an endsplash at one or both ends, check the endsplash kit: since most endsplashes are assembled directly above the end of the cabinet, you generally *subtract* ¾ inch from the length of the countertop on that side.

POST-FORMED LAMINATE COUNTERTOP

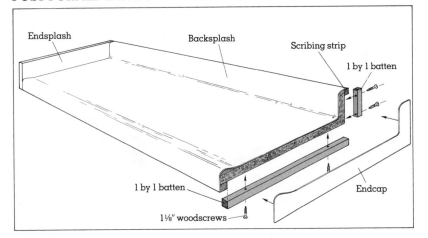

Endsplashes are screwed either directly into the edge of the countertop or into "built-down" wood battens previously attached to the edge, as shown above. Apply silicone sealant to the surfaces to be joined. Holding the endsplash in place with C-clamps, drill pilot holes if needed and drive in the screws.

Endcaps (preshaped strips of matching laminate) are glued to an open end with contact cement or, in some cases, pressed into place with a hot iron. Again, you first may need to build down the edge with wood battens. File the edges of the new strip flush with the top and front edges of the countertop, or use an electric router and laminate-trimming bit.

If your cabinets are U-shaped or L-shaped, you'll need to buy mitered countertop sections or have them cut to order. (It's very difficult to cut accurate miters at home.) The mitered sections should have small slots along the bottom edges. They are connected with take-up or draw bolts, as shown below. Coat the

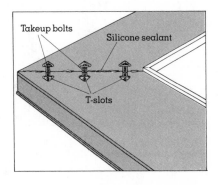

edges with silicone sealant, align the edges carefully, and tighten the bolts. Fasten the adjoining backsplashes together with woodscrews.

Countertops, like cabinets, rarely fit uniformly against the back or side walls because the walls rarely are straight. Usually the back edge of a post-formed countertop comes with a scribing strip that can be trimmed to follow the exact contours of the wall. Follow the instructions for scribing cabinets, detailed on page 109.

Position the countertop on the cabinet frame. Carefully check with a level—across the front and from front to back. Also make sure you can freely open and close the cabinet doors and top drawers with the countertop overhang in place. You may need to add shims or wood blocks around the perimeter and along cross-members of the cabinet top to level or raise the surface.

Fasten the countertop to the cabinets by running screws from below through the cabinet corner gussets or top frame (see drawing, page 108) and through any shims or wood blocks. Use woodscrews just long enough to penetrate ½ inch into the countertop core. Run a bead of silicone sealant along all exposed seams between the countertop and walls; clean up any excess.

If you need to cut a hole for a sink or cooktop in the new countertop, you'll need a keyhole or saber saw, and a drill for pilot holes. See page 121 for more details.

(Continued on next page)

... Cabinets & countertops

SELF-RIMMED LAMINATE COUNTERTOP

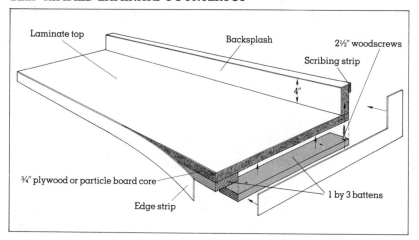

Laminate top
Backsplash
2½" woodscrews
Scribing strip
4"
¾" plywood or particle board core
Edge strip
1 by 3 battens

Self-rimmed laminate countertop. To build your own laminate countertop, you'll need to choose the laminate (¹⁄₁₆-inch thickness is the standard) and cut the core material to size from ¾-inch plywood or high-density particle board.

Build down the edges of the core with 1 by 3 battens (see drawing above). Then proceed to laminate the countertop. Do sides and front strips first, then the top surface, in the following manner:

Measure each surface to be laminated, adding ¼ inch to all dimensions as a margin for error. Mark the cutting line. Score the line with a sharp utility knife; then cut with a fine-toothed saw (face up with a handsaw, face down with a power saw). A laminate cutter is ideal.

Apply contact cement to both the laminate back and core surface to be joined, and allow the cement to dry for 20 to 30 minutes. Carefully check alignment before joining the two; once joined, the laminate can't be moved. Press the laminate into place, using a roller or a rolling pin to ensure even contact.

Use a block plane to trim the laminate flush with the core's edges; then dress it with a file. Or trim with an electric router equipped with a laminate-trimming bit.

Backsplashes or endsplashes should be cut from the same core material as the main countertop, then butt-joined to the countertop with sealant and woodscrews.

Installing ceramic tile countertops

Wall tiles, lighter and thinner than floor tiles, are the normal choice for countertops and backsplashes. Standard sizes range from 3 inches by 3 inches to 4½ inches by 8½ inches, with thicknesses varying from ¼ inch to ⅜ inch.

Preparing the base. Before you can lay tile, it's best to remove any present countertops (see page 108); then install ¾-inch exterior plywood, cut flush with the cabinet top, by screwing it to the cabinet frame from below.

Both the plywood base and the wall surface may need to be primed or sealed before tile is applied. To determine whether you need to prime or seal, read the information on the

adhesive container or ask your supplier.

Planning your layout. Before you start laying tile, you must decide how you want to trim the countertop edge and the sink. For ideas, see the drawing below.

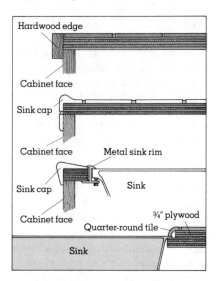

Hardwood edge
Cabinet face
Sink cap
Cabinet face
Metal sink rim
Sink cap
Sink
Cabinet face
¾" plywood
Quarter-round tile
Sink

If you decide to use wood trim, seal the wood and attach it to the cabinet face with finishing nails. When in place, the wood strip's top edge should be positioned at the same height as the finished tile. A recessed sink, commonly used with tile countertops, is also installed at this time (see page 121).

On the front edge of your plywood base, locate and mark the point where the center of the sink or the

HOW TO SET COUNTERTOP TILES

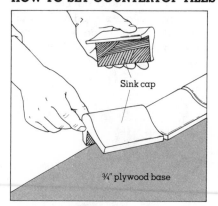

Sink cap
¾" plywood base

First, set edge tiles in place, starting from the center line, after buttering the backs with adhesive.

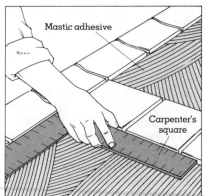

Mastic adhesive
Carpenter's square

Next, install field tiles. Use a square to keep the tiles perpendicular to the edge trim.

midpoint of a blank countertop will be. Lay the edge tiles out on the countertop, starting from your mark. Some tiles have small ceramic lugs molded onto their edges to keep spacing equal; if your tiles don't, use plastic spacers, available from your tile supplier.

Carefully position the rest of the "field" tiles on the countertop. Observing the layout, make any necessary adjustments to eliminate narrow cuts or difficult fits.

If the countertop will have a backsplash or will turn a corner, be sure to figure the cove or corner tiles into your layout.

Mark reference points of your layout on the plywood base to help you re-create it later; then remove the tile.

Setting the tiles. Set all trim tiles before spreading adhesive for the field tiles. Type I mastic, water-resistant and easy to use, is the best adhesive choice for countertops.

Butter the back of each front-edge tile and press into place, aligning it with the reference marks. If your edge trim consists of two tile rows, set the vertical piece first.

Next, butter any back cove tiles and set them against the wall. If you've installed a recessed sink, next lay the sink trim. Be sure to caulk between the sink and the base before setting the trim. If you're using quarter-round trim, you can either

miter the corners or use special corner pieces available with some patterns.

Next, spread adhesive over a section of the countertop (for tools and techniques, see page 116). Begin laying the field tiles, working from front to back. Cut tiles to fit, as necessary. As you lay the tiles, check the alignment frequently with a carpenter's square.

To set the tiles and level their faces, slide a 1-foot-square scrap of cloth-covered plywood over them and tap the scrap with a hammer.

Now set the backsplash, beginning one grout joint space above the cove tiles or countertop tiles. Cover the backsplash area with adhesive; for a better grip, you can also butter the back of each tile.

Unless you're tiling up to an overhead cabinet or window sill, use bullnose tiles for the last row. If a wall contains electrical switches or plug-in outlets, you can cut tiles in two and use tile nippers to nip out a hole.

Applying the grout. Remove any spacers, and clean the tile surface and grout joints until they're free of adhesive. Allow mastic adhesive to set for 24 hours before grouting the joints. For details on grouting tools and techniques, see page 117.

After grouting, wait at least 2 weeks for the grout to cure; then apply a recommended sealer.

Installing synthetic marble countertops

Some types of synthetic marble can be cut, shaped, and joined using woodworking techniques, though you will need power tools and carbide-tipped blades to do the job well.

Synthetic marble used for countertops usually ranges from ½ inch to ¾ inch thick. The ½-inch thickness must be continuously supported by the cabinet frame or by closely spaced plywood blocks. If you're installing a sink, you should add cross-members to the cabinet frame for support.

When you cut the slab, be sure it is firmly supported throughout its length. Mark and cut on the back side. Protect the cutting line with masking tape.

The countertop can be edged with wood trim, strips of synthetic marble, or a combination. If you're skilled with an electric router, you can shape a variety of custom edge treatments in the marble. Be sure to apply petroleum jelly to adjacent surfaces to guard against scratches.

Both wood and marble edges and backsplashes are glued and clamped in place until dry. When joining wood to marble, use neoprene adhesive; for marble-to-marble joints, use an adhesive recommended by the manufacturer.

Before installing the countertop, run a bead of neoprene adhesive around the top of the cabinet frame and on top of any cross-members or plywood blocks. With helpers, lower the countertop into place, and press down to seat it in the adhesive. Apply silicone sealant between the countertop and walls.

HOW TO SET BACKSPLASH TILES

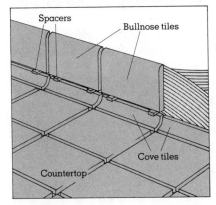

Align joints of backsplash tiles with tiles on the countertop; finish the top with bullnose tiles.

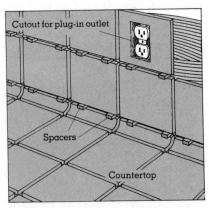

To fit tiles around plug-in outlets, cut a hole in the tile or cut the tile in two and nibble out a hole.

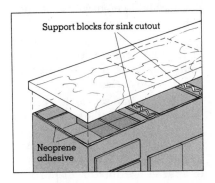

Flooring

Flooring manufacturers are continually revising their wares—improving selection, and making floors easier to care for and easier to install.

Two primary requirements for a kitchen floor are moisture-resistance and durability. Resilient sheet flooring, ceramic tile, and properly sealed hardwood strips all make good choices. Resilient flooring is the simplest of the three to install, especially if this is the only kitchen improvement you're planning. Ideally, both ceramic tile and hardwood strip floors are installed when cabinets, countertops, fixtures, doors, and appliances are not in the room.

The information in this section applies to floors supported by a standard subfloor, with joists or beams below (see drawing, page 83). If you're working with a cement slab, you may have to make special preparations to ensure that it's dry. For specific instructions, see the *Sunset* book *Do-It-Yourself Flooring.*

Resilient sheet flooring

Resilient sheet flooring can be laid in adhesive or placed loosely on the floor like wall-to-wall carpet. Though a few types are available in widths up to 12 feet, most sheet flooring is 6 feet wide and may require seaming.

Preparing the subfloor. Old resilient floors and wood floors both make acceptable bases for new resilient sheets, provided their surfaces are completely smooth and level. Old resilient flooring must be the solid not the cushioned type, and firmly bonded to the subfloor. Uneven wood floors may need a rough sanding (see page 119). Both types must be thoroughly cleaned, with loose tiles or boards secured in place.

Old flooring in poor condition or flooring of ceramic tile or masonry should be removed, if possible, down to the subfloor.

If it is impossible to remove without damaging the subfloor, or if the subfloor is in poor condition, cover the old flooring with ¼-inch underlayment-grade plywood, untempered hardboard, or particle board. Leave a ¹⁄₁₆-inch gap between panels to allow for later expansion. Fasten the panels down with 3-penny ring-shank or 4-penny cement-coated nails spaced 3 inches apart along the edges and 6 inches apart across the face of each panel.

Planning the new floor. Take exact measurements of the kitchen floor, and make a scale drawing on graph paper. Include the locations of any irregularities in the room: base cabinets, island cabinets, closets, or pantries. If your room is very irregular, you may want to make a full-size paper pattern of the floor instead of the scale drawing.

To cover a large area, it may be necessary to make a seam between two pieces. Looking at your floor plan or pattern, determine how to combine sheets so you can cover the floor with the minimum amount of material. If the flooring is patterned, you'll need enough extra to match the pattern at the seams.

Installing flooring without seams. The most critical step in laying sheet flooring is making the first rough cuts accurately.

Unroll the flooring in a large room or in a clean garage or basement. Transfer the floor plan—or paper pattern—directly onto the top of the flooring, using chalk or a water-soluble felt-tip pen, a carpenter's square, and a long straightedge.

Using a linoleum or utility knife or heavy-duty scissors, cut the flooring roughly 3 inches over-size on all sides. The excess will be trimmed away after the flooring has been positioned.

Cut 3" extra

Actual room size

If adhesive is required with your flooring, it can either be spread over the entire subfloor or, depending on the type of adhesive, spread in steps as the flooring is unrolled. Check the adhesive's "open-time"—the time it takes to dry.

Remove the baseboards and moldings from walls and cabinet fronts. Carry the roll of flooring into the kitchen and lay the longest edge against the longest wall, allowing the 3-inch excess to curl up the wall. The flooring should also curl up each adjoining wall. If the entire floor has been covered with adhesive, slowly roll the flooring out across the room. Take care to set the flooring firmly into the adhesive as you proceed. When you finish, start at the center of the room and work out any air bubbles that may remain. You can use a rolling pin for this, or rent a floor roller.

Installing flooring with seams. Transfer your floor plan or paper pattern to the flooring as described above. On flooring with a decorative pattern, be sure to leave the margins necessary to match the pattern at the seam on adjoining sheets (see below). If your flooring has a simulated grout or mortar joint, plan to cut the seam along the midpoint of the printed joint.

Cut the piece that requires the most intricate fitting first. If using adhesive, spread it on the subfloor as directed, stopping 8 or 9 inches from the seam. Then position the sheet on the floor. If you're not using adhesive, simply put the first sheet in place.

Next cut the second sheet of flooring and position it to overlap the first sheet by at least 2 inches; make sure the design is perfectly aligned. Again, if using adhesive, stop 8 or 9 inches from the seam; if not, position, the second sheet carefully, then secure it to the subfloor with two or three strips of double-faced tape.

When the flooring is in position, trim away excess material at each end of the seam in a half-moon shape so the ends butt against the wall (see drawing above right).

HOW TO MAKE SEAMS

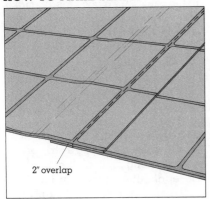

Overlap sheets at least 2 inches; be certain the design is perfectly aligned.

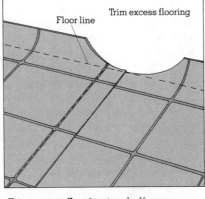

Trim excess flooring in a half-moon shape so the ends butt against the wall.

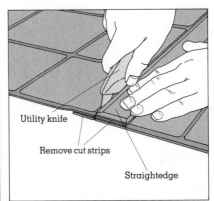

Cut down through both sheets along a straightedge, then remove the cut strips.

Using a steel straightedge and a sharp utility knife, make a straight cut—about ½ to ⅝ inch from the edge of the top sheet—down through both sheets of flooring. Lift up the flooring and spread adhesive under the seam—or if you're not using adhesive, apply a long piece of double-faced tape beneath the seam. Clean the area around the seam, using the appropriate solvent for your adhesive. Fuse the two pieces with a recommended seam sealer.

Trimming to fit. You'll need to make a series of relief cuts at all inside and outside corners to allow the flooring to lie flat on the floor.

At inside corners, gradually trim away the excess with diagonal cuts until the flooring lies flat (see drawing below). At outside corners, start

at the top of the lapped-up flooring and cut straight down to the point where the wall and floor meet.

After you cut the corners, remove the material lapped up against the walls. Using an 18 to 24-inch-long piece of 2 by 4, press the flooring into a right angle where the floor and wall join.

Lay a heavy metal straightedge along the wall and trim the flooring with a utility knife, leaving a gap of about ⅛ inch between the edge of the flooring and the wall. This will allow the material to expand without buckling; the baseboard and/or shoe molding will cover the gap. If you're planning to attach vinyl wall base (see below), be sure the base will overlap the edge of the flooring at least ¼ inch.

The most effective way to hide

an exposed edge around a doorway is to cut away just enough of the door casing to permit the flooring to slide underneath.

Finishing touches. When the new flooring has been cleaned and is flat and well-settled, replace any baseboards that have been removed. Then reattach the shoe molding, leaving a ¹⁄₃₂ to ¹⁄₁₆-inch gap between the flooring and the bottom of the molding. Always drive nails through the molding into the baseboards, never down into the flooring.

Vinyl wall base, an alternative to baseboards and molding, is fastened directly to the wall or base cabinets with adhesive; the lower edge rests on, but is not attached to, the flooring. Finally, finish your new floor as recommended.

(Continued on next page)

HOW TO TRIM FLOORING

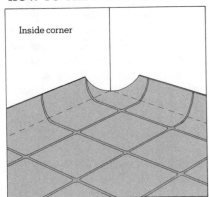

Where flooring turns an inside corner, cut the excess with diagonal cuts.

At outside corner, cut straight down to the point where wall and floor meet.

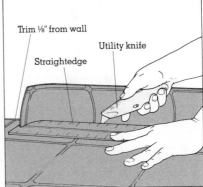

Trim flooring, leaving a ⅛" gap between the edge and the wall.

... Flooring

Ceramic tile floors

You can install a ceramic tile floor in a three-step operation: lay evenly spaced tiles in a bed of adhesive atop a smooth, dry, and rigid subfloor; fill the joint spaces between tiles with grout; and seal the floor for durability and easy cleaning. Glazed tiles, Type I mastic adhesive, and cement-based grout are probably the best materials for the kitchen do-it-yourselfer.

Preparing the subfloor. If at all possible, remove old flooring before installing new ceramic tiles. Not only does this enable you to examine the subfloor and make any necessary repairs, but it should also make the new floor level with floors in adjacent rooms. But if your old resilient (solid, not cushioned), ceramic tile, wood, or masonry flooring is level and in good repair, it can be successfully covered with tile. Your tile dealer can recommend the best adhesive and method of application.

To prepare a plywood subfloor, make certain that all panels are securely attached to the joists. If the subfloor is constructed from individual 4 or 6-inch boards, be sure that each board is securely attached. Drive any protruding nails flush with the surface.

To prevent a board subfloor from warping, or if the plywood subfloor is in poor condition, you'll have to install a new layer over the old before laying tile. Use exterior or underlayment-grade plywood or particle board at least ⅜ inch thick, and leave a ¹⁄₁₆-inch gap between adjacent panels. Fasten the panels with 6-penny ring-shank nails spaced 6 inches apart. Where possible, drive nails through the panels into the floor joists.

Regardless of your subfloor material, you may need to use a sealer before applying adhesive. Check your adhesive for instructions.

Establish working lines. The key to laying straight rows of tile is to establish proper working lines. You can begin either at the center of the room or at one wall.

If two adjoining walls meet at an exact right angle, start laying tiles along one wall. This method means that fewer border tiles need to be cut; it also allows you to work without stepping on rows previously set.

To check for square corners and straight walls, place a tile tightly into each corner. Stretch a chalkline between the corners of each pair of tiles; pull the line tight and snap each line. Variations in the distance between chalklines and walls will reveal any irregularities in the walls. You can ignore variations as slight as the width of a grout joint. With a carpenter's square, check the intersection of lines in each corner of the room.

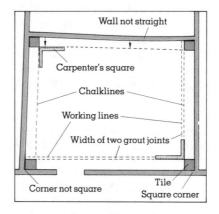

Assuming that your walls are reasonably straight, you can begin laying tile at any straight wall adjoining a straight corner. Snap a new chalkline parallel to the original line and approximately two grout joint widths closer to the center of the room (see drawing above). Lay a similar line, at a right angle to the first, along the adjoining wall. Then nail a batten (wood straightedge) along each of these working lines.

If you can't find a square corner, begin at the center of the room. Locate the center point on each of two opposite walls, and snap a chalkline between the two points. Then find the centers of the other two walls and stretch your chalkline at right angles to the first line; snap the line only after you've used your carpenter's square to determine that the two lines cross at a precise right angle.

Whether you begin at a wall or in the center, it's a good idea to make a dry run before you actually set the tiles in adhesive. Lay the tiles out on the lines, allowing proper spacing for grout joints. Try to determine the best layout while keeping the number of tiles to be cut to a minimum.

Setting the tiles. Using a notched trowel, start spreading a strip of adhesive along one of the battens. Cover about a square yard at first, or the area you can comfortably tile before the adhesive begins to set.

Using a gentle twisting motion, place the first tile in the corner formed by the two battens. With the same motion, place a second tile alongside the first. To establish the proper width for the grout joint, use molded plastic spacers. Continue laying tiles along the batten until the row is complete. Start each new row at the same end as the first. If you're working from the center of the room, follow one of the patterns shown below.

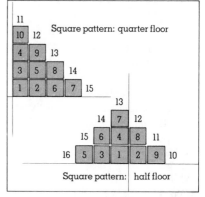

As the tiles are laid, set a piece of carpet-wrapped wood over the tiles; tap it with a mallet or hammer to "beat in" the tiles. Keep checking with a carpenter's square or straightedge to make sure each course is straight. Wiggle any stray tiles back into position while the adhesive is still flexible.

When you're ready to install border tiles, carefully remove the battens. Measure the remaining spaces individually, subtract the width of two grout joints, and mark each tile for any necessary cuts.

HOW TO SET CERAMIC FLOOR TILES

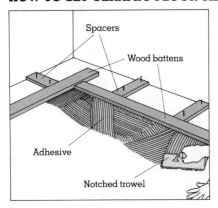

Nail batten boards at right angles, flush with the working lines. Then spread adhesive alongside one batten with a notched trowel.

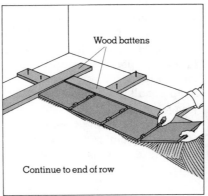

Begin placing tiles from the corner formed by the battens, using spacers to maintain the width of the grout joint. Continue to the end of the first row.

Start each new row at the same end as the first row. To set tiles in adhesive, slide a beating block (padded wood block) over the tiles while tapping it with a hammer.

You can cut tile with a tile cutter rented from your tile supplier; or you can (A) score tile with a glass cutter and straightedge, then (B) press it down evenly over a ¼-inch dowel (see below). To cut irregular shapes, use a tile nipper; first score the cutting lines with a glass cutter.

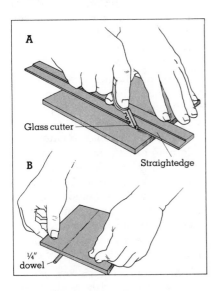

After all the tiles are placed, remove any spacers and clean the tile surface so it's completely free of adhesive. Before applying grout, allow the tiles to set properly—about 24 hours with mastic adhesives.

Applying grout. Grout can be applied liberally around glazed tiles. Grouting unglazed tiles requires more care, since the grout may stain the tile's surface. Be sure to read the manufacturer's recommendations.

Using a rubber-faced float or squeegee, apply grout to the surface of the tile. Force the grout into the joints so they're completely filled; make sure no air pockets remain. Scrape off excess grout with the float, working diagonally across the tiles.

Soak a sponge in clear water and wring it out. Wipe the tiles with a circular motion, removing any remaining grout, until the joints are smooth and level with the tiles. Rinse and wring out the sponge frequently.

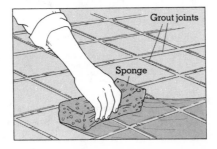

When the tiles are clean, let the grout dry for about 30 minutes. By then, any film of grout left on the tile will have formed a light haze; immediately polish it off with a soft cloth. Smooth the grout joints with a jointer, striking tool, or toothbrush.

Finishing touches. Most grouts take at least 2 weeks to cure. You'll need to damp-cure a cement-based grout by covering the newly installed floor with plastic. Leave the plastic in place for 24 hours; then remove it and allow the grout to cure thoroughly. Stay off the tile until cured.

Once the grout has fully cured, seal it and the tile with a silicone or lacquer-base sealer recommended by your tile supplier.

Wood strip flooring

Wood strip flooring, the most popular "hardwood" floor, is made up of narrow boards with tongue-and-groove edges and ends, laid in random lengths.

You can buy finished or unfinished wood strips. The latter is the best choice for kitchen flooring—the ability to seal joints between the strips is a must for water-resistance.

Though widths and thicknesses vary, the most common strip flooring for finishing in place is ¾ inch or $^{25}/_{32}$ inch thick, with a face width of 2¼ inches.

(Continued on next page)

... Flooring

Preparing the subfloor. The subfloor preparation can be more demanding than putting in the new flooring. Moisture is the number one enemy of wood floors; you must ensure that the subfloor is completely dry and will remain dry. Any crawlspace below the floor must also be properly ventilated and protected from moisture.

Though it's possible to lay wood flooring over an old wood floor that's structurally sound and perfectly level, you may need to remove the old flooring to get down to the subfloor and make necessary repairs or install underlayment. In the long run, this usually provides the most reliable base for your new floor.

Check the exposed subfloor for loose boards or loose plywood panels. If planks are badly bowed and cannot be flattened by nailing, give the floor a rough sanding with a floor sander (see page 119) or cover it with ⅜ or ½-inch plywood or particle board. Fasten down ⅜-inch material with 3-penny ring-shank or cement-coated nails; for ½-inch material, use 4-penny ring-shank or 5-penny cement-coated nails. Space nails 6 inches apart across the surface of the panels.

New or old, the base for the new floor should be cleaned thoroughly, then covered with a layer of 15-pound asphalt-saturated felt (butting seams) or soft resin paper (overlapping seams 4 inches).

As you put the felt or paper in place, use a straightedge or a chalkline to mark the center of each joist on the covering. The lines will serve as reference points when you attach the new flooring.

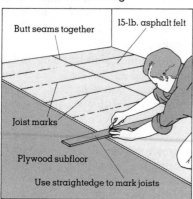

Butt seams together
15-lb. asphalt felt
Joist marks
Plywood subfloor
Use straightedge to mark joists

Planning the new floor. For a trouble-free installation, the first course you lay must be parallel to the center of the kitchen.

Measure the width of the room in several spots and locate the center line as accurately as possible. Snap a chalkline to mark the center, your primary reference point.

Next, measuring from the center line, lay out and snap another chalkline about ½ inch from the wall you're using as a starting point.

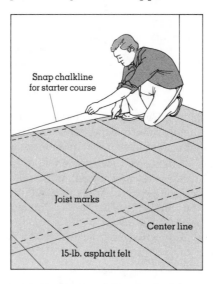

Snap chalkline for starter course
Joist marks
Center line
15-lb. asphalt felt

In a kitchen that's obviously irregular in shape, locate the center line as closely as possible and begin laying the first row of flooring from that point. A special wood strip called a *spline* is used to join two back-to-back grooved boards along the center line.

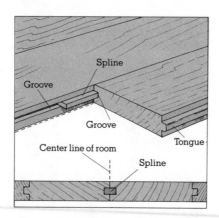

Spline
Groove
Groove
Center line of room
Tongue
Spline

Installing the flooring. When starting from the wall, you may need to trim a few boards at the outset. It's important that your first row of flooring line up properly while keeping the ½-inch distance from the wall. If you're starting from the center of an irregular room, the trimming will be done later when you reach the walls.

Tongue-and-groove strip flooring is attached by nailing at an angle through the tongues, where nail heads won't show. (This is called "blind-nailing.") To ensure a tight floor, install strips perpendicular to joists.

You can make a perfectly acceptable installation using basic hand tools, but a nailer—available from most tool rental companies—will speed up the work. Similarly, boards can be neatly cut with a back saw and miter box, but a radial-arm or table saw saves time and labor.

If you're starting along the wall, the first row of boards should be secured by face-nailing; the nails will be covered later with shoe molding. Predrill the boards with holes slightly smaller than the diameter of your nails.

When beginning at the center of an irregularly shaped room, you can start right off by blind-nailing through the tongues—with the nailer, if you have one.

Lay out boards six or seven rows ahead. This will help you plan an effective and attractive pattern. Stagger end joints so that no joint is closer than 6 inches to a joint in an adjoining row of boards. Leave approximately ½ inch between each end piece and the wall. As a general rule, no end piece should be shorter than 8 inches. When laying flooring over plywood or particle board, avoid placing the end joints in the flooring directly over joints in the subfloor.

As you place each row, move a block of wood along the leading edge of the flooring you've just put down, and give it a sharp rap with a mallet or hammer before you drive each nail. To avoid damaging the tongues, cut a groove in the block to accommodate the tongue, or use a short length of flooring.

Since you won't have enough space to use a nailer until you are several rows from the wall, you'll

HOW TO LAY WOOD STRIP FLOORING

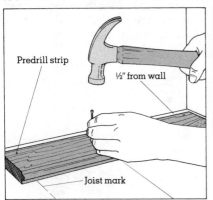

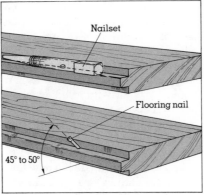

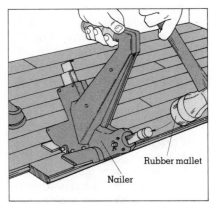

Predrill holes slightly smaller than the nail diameter, then face-nail the first course from the wall.

Nail first few rows by hand—start with a hammer, then drive the nail home with a nailset laid sideways along the tongue.

Once there's working room, drive nails with a nailer and rubber mallet; the nailer automatically drives nails flush.

have to nail the first courses by hand. By continuing to predrill holes for the nails, you can keep nails at the proper angle—45° to 50° from the floor—and help prevent splitting. Take care not to crush the upper edges of the boards. Instead of using your hammer to drive nails flush, leave the heads exposed; then place a nailset sideways over each nail along the top of the tongue, and tap the nailset with your hammer. Use the nailset's tip to drive the nail flush.

Once you have laid and nailed the first few rows by hand, you can begin to secure the flooring with a nailer, which automatically countersinks all the nails it drives.

When you reach the last few rows, you'll find it difficult to blind-nail the boards. Predrill holes and face-nail them. The final strip of flooring must be placed to leave a ½-inch gap between the flooring and the wall. If you're lucky, a standard board will fit. If not, you'll have to rip several boards down to the proper width.

If your new floor creates a change of level from one room to the next, smooth the transition with a rounded reducer strip.

Finishing touches. An unfinished floor will have to be sanded and finished. Most equipment rental companies offer the necessary heavy-duty equipment. The workhorse of this job is the floor (drum)

sander; look for a machine with a tilt-up lever that makes it possible to raise the drum off the floor without lifting the machine.

You'll also need an edging machine, a type of disk sander necessary for areas (next to a wall, for example) that can't be reached with a drum sander. A hand block and sandpaper are useful for corners and other tight spots.

When sanding a floor, you may also need a hammer and nailset to drive down protruding nail heads, and wood putty to fill holes, dents, and gouges.

Typically, three sandings—called "cuts"—using three grades of sandpaper are needed to prepare a floor for finishing. Floor sanding equipment, especially the unwieldy drum sander, must be operated with great care to avoid irrep-

arable damage to the new floor. For sanding techniques and procedures, see the *Sunset* book *Do-It-Yourself Flooring,* or ask your flooring supplier for recommendations.

Polyurethane has become today's dominant wood floor finish. It provides a hard, plasticlike surface that's impermeable to water and easy to care for.

To apply polyurethane, start with a clean brush along the walls and around obstacles. Then use a long-handled paint roller with a mohair cover to apply the finish evenly over the rest of the floor.

At least two (and preferably three) coats of polyurethane are the rule in the kitchen. Between coats, use a floor buffer equipped with #2 steel wool to smooth the surface. Corners and other hard-to-reach spots should be smoothed by hand.

FLOOR FINISHING TOOLS

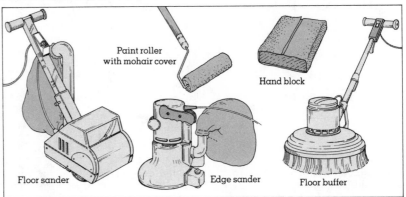

Fixtures & appliances

Disk faucets, double self-rimmed sinks, built-in dishwashers, microwave ovens ... the array of styles, colors, and special features available in kitchen fixtures and appliances can be bewildering. For help in making your selection, see pages 37–43.

Fortunately for the do-it-yourselfer, most variations of the basic fixtures and appliances are installed in a similar manner. The following pages cover the fundamentals. Specific instructions should accompany each unit (check before purchase); follow the manufacturer's instructions if they differ from those below.

Many fixtures and appliances can be easily connected to an existing sink drain or electrical outlet. But before you make any purchase, be sure your home's plumbing and electrical systems can handle the new load. For a discussion of plumbing and electrical systems, their limitations, and applicable codes, see "Plumbing basics," pages 90–92, and "Electrical basics," pages 93–97.

Sometimes the greatest challenge of replacing a major appliance such as a refrigerator, is transporting the old one from the site and bringing in the new one. Always plan your route in advance ("Do we need to remove a door? How will we get it down the steps?"), and have adequate help on hand. An appliance dolly can be indispensable.

Installing a faucet

Most modern kitchen faucets are the deck-mounted type, seated on the rear of the sink and secured from below. When shopping for a replacement, you'll find the selection staggering. You can choose from a lineup of single-handled washerless faucets—valve, disk, ball, and cartridge—and styles ranging from antique reproductions to futuristic compression models. All are interchangeable as long as the new faucet's inlet shanks are spaced to fit the holes on the sink.

If you still have old-fashioned wall-mounted faucets, you face a different decision: either buy an updated style, or switch to a deck-mounted type. Switching types adds several steps to the installation process; at the minimum, you'll need to reroute pipes from the wall into the kitchen cabinet and patch the wall. For help with either choice, see the *Sunset* book *Basic Plumbing Illustrated*.

Removing a deck-mounted faucet. Begin by shutting off the water supply, either at the shutoff valves on both hot and cold water supply lines or (if you don't have shutoff valves) at the main house shutoff near the water meter. Then drain the pipes by opening the faucet or faucets.

Use a wrench to unfasten the couplings that attach the supply tubing to the shutoff valves. Since

space is cramped under the sink, use a basin wrench to loosen and remove the locknuts and washers on both faucet inlet shanks.

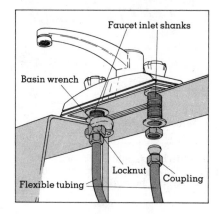

On a kitchen sink with a spray hose attachment, use the basin wrench to undo the locknuts connecting the hose to the faucet body and the hose nipple. Then lift the faucet away from the sink.

Installing the new faucet. Clean the surface of the sink where the new faucet will sit. Most faucets come with a rubber gasket on the bottom; if yours doesn't, apply plumber's putty to the base.

Set the faucet in position, simultaneously feeding the flexible supply tubing, if attached, down through the middle sink hole. (If your new faucet has no tubing included, buy two lengths of tubing and attach them at this point.) Press the

HOW TO INSTALL FAUCETS

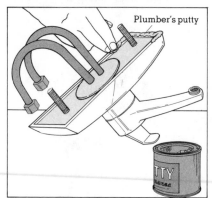

Apply plumber's putty to the bottom edge of the faucet body if there's no gasket to seal it to the sink's surface.

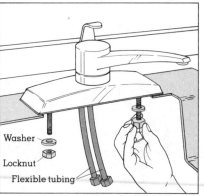

Set the faucet in place, threading supply tubes through the sink hole; then tighten the locknuts.

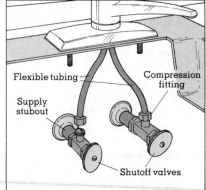

Attach flexible tubing to the shutoff valves, using appropriate compression fittings.

faucet onto the sink's surface. Place the washers and locknuts on the faucet inlet shanks; tighten them with a basin wrench. Attach a spray hose according to the manufacturer's instructions.

Run the flexible tubing to the shutoff valves, gently bending the tubing as necessary, and connect it using compression fittings. (If you'd like to install shutoff valves in your system, see the *Sunset* book *Basic Plumbing Illustrated*.)

Installing a sink

A deck-mounted kitchen sink fits into a specially cut hole in the countertop. If you're simply replacing a sink, you can choose any model the same size as the present sink, or *larger*; if it's a new installation, you'll have to make the sink cutout first.

Three basic sink types prevail: frame-rimmed, self-rimmed, and

SINK DRAIN ELEMENTS

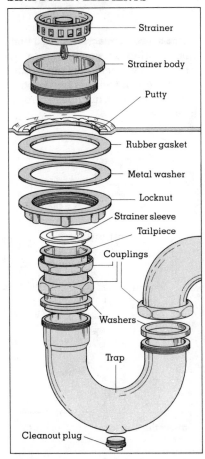

Strainer

Strainer body

Putty

Rubber gasket

Metal washer

Locknut

Strainer sleeve

Tailpiece

Couplings

Washers

Trap

Cleanout plug

unrimmed. A frame-rimmed sink has a surrounding metal channel that holds the sink to the countertop; a self-rimmed sink has a molded overlap that's supported by the countertop cutout; and an un-rimmed sink is recessed beneath the countertop cutout and held in place by metal clips.

Removing an old sink. First shut off the water supply at the shutoff valves on both hot and cold water supply pipes; if you don't have shutoff valves, turn off the water at the main house shutoff. Then drain the pipes by opening both faucets, and disconnect the supply pipes as described on page 120. You'll also need to disconnect the drain trap from the sink's strainer assembly. Loosen the couplings that hold the tailpiece to the strainer assembly, and the tailpiece to the trap. Push the tailpiece down into the trap.

From below the sink, remove any clamps or lugs holding it to the countertop. If necessary, break the putty seal by forcing the sink free.

Making a sink cutout. For a new installation, trace either a template (included with the new sink) or the bottom edge of the frame onto the exact spot where the sink will sit. Typically, 1½ to 2 inches is left between the edge of the cutout and the front edge of the countertop. Drill pilot holes in each corner of the outline, and insert a saber saw into one of the holes to make the cutout.

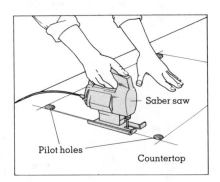

Saber saw

Pilot holes

Countertop

Installing the new sink. It's best to mount the faucet and hook up the strainer assembly before installing the new sink in the countertop.

To install a strainer assembly, first apply a bead of plumber's putty to the underlip of the strainer body, then press it down into the sink opening. If the strainer is held in place by a locknut, place the rubber gasket and metal washer over the strainer body, and tighten by hand. Hold the strainer from above while you snug up the locknut, preferably with a spud wrench. If the strainer is held in place by a retainer, fit the retainer over the strainer body and tighten all three screws. Attach the tailpiece with a coupling.

For a frame-rimmed sink, apply a ring of plumber's putty around the top edge of the sink. Fasten the frame to the sink, following the manufacturer's instructions; some frames attach with metal corner clamps, others with metal extension tabs that bend around the sink lip. Wipe off excess putty.

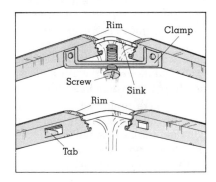

Rim

Clamp

Screw

Sink

Rim

Tab

Before installing a deck-mounted sink of any style, apply a ½-inch-wide strip of putty or silicone sealant along the edge of the countertop opening. Set the sink into the cutout, pressing it down. Smooth excess putty.

Anchor the sink from below at 6 or 8-inch intervals, using any clamps or lugs provided. Hook up the supply pipes and drain trap.

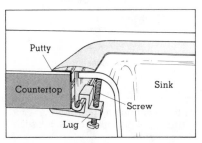

Putty

Countertop

Sink

Screw

Lug

(Continued on next page)

... Fixtures & appliances

Installing a garbage disposer

Installing a disposer takes a few hours, but the basic connection is not difficult. Most units fit the standard 3½ or 4-inch drain outlets of kitchen sinks and mount somewhat like a sink strainer (see page 121).

Plumbing a disposer involves altering the sink trap to fit the unit. If your model has direct wiring, you must run electrical cable to a nearby junction box or other power source (see pages 93–97 for information). Plug-in disposers require a 120-volt grounded (three-prong) outlet under the sink, and a separate wall switch adjacent to the sink.

Before installing a disposer, check plumbing codes for any restrictions.

Removing a strainer or disposer. If you're adding a disposer for the first time, first disconnect the sink strainer assembly. Start by removing the tailpiece and trap (see page 121); then disassemble the strainer components and lift them out of the sink. Clean away any old putty or sealing gaskets around the opening.

If you're replacing a disposer, first turn off the electricity (see page 93); then unplug the unit or disconnect the wiring. Loosen the screws on the mounting ring assembly and

remove the parts; finally, remove the sink flange from above.

Mounting the disposer. The disposer comes with its own sink flange and mounting assembly. Run a bead of plumber's putty around the sink opening and seat the flange. Then, working from below, slip the gasket, mounting rings, and snap ring up onto the neck of the flange. The snap ring should fit firmly into a groove on the sink flange to hold things in place temporarily.

Uniformly tighten the slotted screws in the mounting rings until the gasket fits snugly against the bottom of the flange. Remove any excess putty from around the flange.

Attach the drain elbow to the disposer. Lift the disposer into place, aligning the holes in the disposer's flange with the slotted screws in the mounting rings. Rotate the disposer so that the drain elbow lines up with the drainpipe. Tighten the nuts securely onto the slotted screws to ensure a good seal.

Making the hookups. Fit the coupling and washer onto the drain elbow. Add an elbow fitting on the other end of the trap to adjust to the drainpipe. You may need to shorten the drainpipe to make the connection. Tighten all connections, and

run water down through the disposer to check for leaks.

At this point, either plug the disposer into a grounded outlet (see pages 96–97) or shut off the power and wire the unit directly, following the manufacturer's instructions. Then turn the power back on. To be safe, test the unit for proper grounding (for techniques, see the *Sunset* book *Basic Home Wiring Illustrated*).

Installing a dishwasher

A built-in dishwasher requires three connections; hot water supply, drainpipe fitting, and a 120-volt, 20-amp, grounded plug-in outlet. (For basic electrical information, see pages 93–97.)

Local codes may require that you also install a venting device, called an air gap, on the sink or countertop. Some municipalities require a permit and an inspection when a built-in dishwasher is installed; check before you begin the work.

Making new connections. For a first-time installation, you'll need to tap into the hot water supply pipe under the sink, and into either the garbage disposer or sink drainpipe for proper drainage.

HOW TO PLUMB A GARBAGE DISPOSER

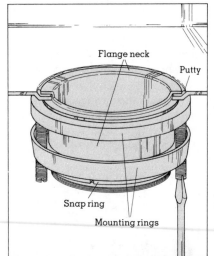

Attach mounting rings, with gasket and snap ring, to the sink flange; tighten the slotted screws.

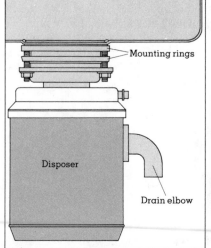

Line up the drain elbow on the disposer so it's directly opposite the drainpipe; tighten nuts onto the slotted screws.

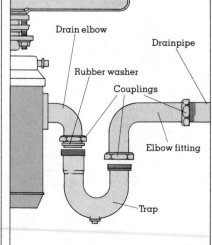

Connect the trap to the disposer's drain elbow and to the elbow fitting on the drainpipe.

Begin by shutting off the water supply, either at the shutoff valves under the sink or at the main house shutoff. Drain the supply pipes by turning on the sink faucets. Cut into the hot water supply pipe and install a tee fitting. (If you need a course in pipefitting techniques, see the *Sunset* book *Basic Plumbing Illustrated*.) Run flexible copper or plastic tubing to the location of the water inlet valve on the dishwasher. To simplify future repairs, install a shutoff valve along the tubing.

Your dishwasher can drain either into the sink drain above the trap or into a garbage disposer. For use with a sink drain, you'll need to buy a threaded waste tee fitting (see drawing below).

To install a waste tee, remove the sink tailpiece (see page 121) and insert the waste tee into the trap. Cut the tailpiece so it fits between the waste tee and the sink strainer assembly. Reattach the tailpiece, and clamp the dishwasher drain hose onto the waste tee fitting.

If you already have (or are installing) a garbage disposer, plan to attach the dishwasher drain hose to the disposer drain fitting on the disposer's side. First turn off the electrical circuit that controls the disposer. Then use a screwdriver to punch out the knockout plug inside the fitting. Clamp the dishwasher drain hose to the fitting.

To prevent a backup of waste water into the dishwasher, make a gradual loop with the drain hose to the height of the dishwasher's top before making the connection. If you're required to install an air gap instead of the loop, insert the air gap into the predrilled hole found on some sinks, or into a hole you've drilled at the back of the countertop. Screw the air gap tight from below.

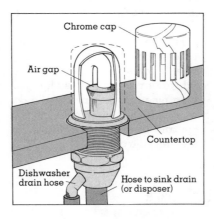

Run one length of hose from the dishwasher to the air gap, and another from the air gap to the waste tee or disposer.

Removing an old dishwasher. If you're simply replacing a dishwasher, the connections should already be made. But you'll have to disconnect and remove the old unit before installing the new one.

First, unfasten any screws or brackets anchoring the unit to the countertop or the floor. Turn off electrical power to the circuit controlling the dishwasher; then shut off the water supply. Disconnect the supply hookup and the drain hose from the dishwasher. With a helper, pull the unit forward to gain access to the electrical connection (unless it's simply under the sink). If the dishwasher is the plug-in type, you're in luck. If it was wired directly, disconnect the wires from the dishwasher.

Completing the installation. Plug in the new dishwasher, then slide it into place. To add a new plug-in outlet, see pages 96–97, or consult a professional electrician. Complete the supply and drain hookups according to the manufacturer's instructions.

Once it's hooked up, level the dishwasher by adjusting the height of the legs. Anchor the unit to the underside of the countertop with any screws provided.

(Continued on next page)

HOW TO CONNECT A DISHWASHER

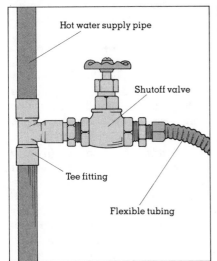

Install a tee fitting and shutoff valve in the hot water supply pipe, then run flexible tubing to the dishwasher.

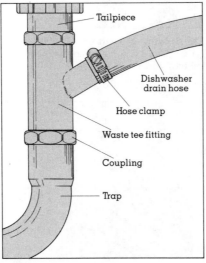

To drain into a sink trap, add a threaded waste tee fitting between tailpiece and trap.

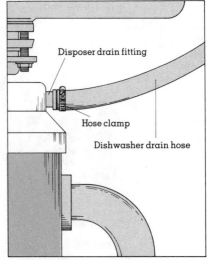

To drain into a garbage disposer, connect a dishwasher drain hose to the disposer's drain fitting.

. . . Fixtures & appliances

Installing a hot water dispenser

Easy-to-install hot water dispensers incorporate a stainless steel faucet connected to an under-counter storage tank. The tank, which in turn is connected to a nearby cold water pipe, has an electric heating coil that keeps water at about 200°F—50° hotter than that produced by the average water heater.

Most units plug into a 120-volt grounded outlet installed under the sink. (For electrical details, see pages 93–97.) Some models, though, are directly wired to a grounded junction box.

Positioning the dispenser. Begin by deciding where you want to place the unit. Commonly, the faucet fits in a hole at the rear of the sink rim, or else mounts directly on the countertop. In the latter case, cut a 1¼-inch-diameter hole in your counter-top near the sink rim with a hole saw or electric drill. Following the manufacturer's instructions, attach the dispenser faucet from beneath the sink. Generally, you'll need only to install a nut and washers to hold the faucet.

From inside the sink cabinet, screw the tank mounting bracket to the wall or cabinet back, making sure it's plumb. The bracket should be located about 14 inches below the underside of the countertop. Next, mount the tank on the bracket.

Making the connections. Before plumbing the unit, shut off the water supply and drain the pipes by opening the sink faucets. Many dispensers come with a self-tapping valve. If yours doesn't, tap into the cold water pipe using a saddle tee fitting (see drawing below). To do this, clamp the fitting to the supply pipe and drill a hole through the fitting into the pipe.

If saddle tees aren't permitted in your area, tap in with a standard tee fitting, then install a shutoff valve and reducer fitting for the dispenser's water supply tube. (For pipefitting techniques, see the *Sunset* book *Basic Plumbing Illustrated.*)

Using the compression nuts provided with the unit, attach one incoming water supply tube between the dispenser and the storage tank, and another between the tank and the cold water supply pipe. Turn on the water supply and check for leaks. Plug in the unit—or shut off the power and connect the wires directly, as required. Finally, turn the power on.

Installing a refrigerator

Installing a new refrigerator is easy work—just plug it in to a 120-volt, 20-amp appliance circuit. Your only real challenge will be handling and transporting both the old and the new units.

Disconnecting a refrigerator. When removing the old refrigerator, simply pull it out any way you can to gain access to the plug. If the unit has an automatic icemaker, the fitting attaching the copper supply tubing must be disconnected. Be prepared to remove doors from their hinges, guard rails from stairways, or any other obstructions in the path. Then secure the refrigerator to an appliance dolly and wheel it out.

Positioning a new refrigerator. Wheel the replacement into a position where you can hook up the icemaker, if necessary, and plug the refrigerator in. Finally push it into place and check level. Adjust the level with shims, as necessary.

A refrigerator can be given a "built-in" look—just wrap modular cabinets around it, or install custom-made cabinets. Be sure to allow ½ inch to 1 inch around all sides for easy removal and air circulation. For a different built-in look, face the refrigerator on one side with an end panel to match the cabinetry; panels are available with most modular cabinet lines.

HOW TO HOOK UP A HOT WATER DISPENSER

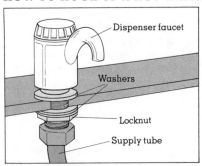

First, secure the dispenser faucet to the sink rim or countertop from below, using nut and washers.

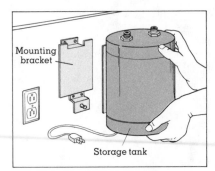

Attach the tank mounting bracket to the wall or cabinet back, then install the storage tank.

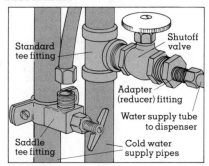

Tap into the cold water supply pipe with a saddle tee or standard tee fitting and shutoff valve.

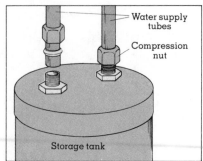

Hook up one supply tube from the dispenser to the storage tank, and one from the tank to the supply pipe.

Installing an icemaker. An automatic icemaker is connected by ¼-inch copper tubing to a cold water supply pipe. To make the connection, use a saddle tee or standard tee fitting and shutoff valve, as detailed under "Installing a hot water dispenser," at left. If the refrigerator can be easily reached from the sink complex, tap in there and drill small access holes through the sides of the base cabinets to route the tubing. If the refrigerator is far from the sink, look for another cold water supply pipe to tap (see pages 90–92 for help).

At the refrigerator end, leave a few extra loops of tubing to help you position the unit. Attach the tubing to the refrigerator with a compression union (see drawing below) or other special fitting, following the manufacturer's instructions.

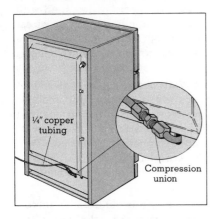

¼" copper tubing

Compression union

Installing a trash compactor

A new trash compactor, like a refrigerator, is simple to hook up—just plug it into a 120-volt, 20-amp grounded outlet. Again, like the refrigerator, your major task is moving it into position.

A typical compactor fits into the same space as a standard 15-inch-wide base cabinet; it can be built in under the countertop, enclosed with an end panel, or used as a freestanding unit.

To install the compactor, move it roughly into position until you can plug in the power cord. Then wrestle it into place (taking care not to scratch the flooring) and level the unit, either by shimming or by adjusting any built-in legs.

Installing cooktops, ranges & wall ovens

Cooking equipment offers you a choice of two energy sources—electricity or gas. In addition it offers three designs—freestanding or "slide-in" range, drop-in range, or a combination of built-in cooktop and separate wall ovens. For a detailed breakdown and evaluation of your options, see pages 37–39.

The only factors limiting your choice are the capacity of your present gas or electrical system, the distance from an existing connection that you plan to move new equipment, and the labor and expense of switching from electricity to gas, or vice versa.

To analyze your present electrical system, see pages 93–94. An electric range, or wall ovens and a separate cooktop, must be powered by an individual 120/240-volt, 50-amp circuit. (The exception is a microwave oven, which requires only 120-volt current.) The power cords on the appliances must be equipped with special 50-amp plugs and attached to special 50-amp outlets. If you need to add a new circuit, see the *Sunset* book *Basic Home Wiring Illustrated*, or consult a licensed electrician.

For a discussion of gas system basics, see page 92. A gas range can usually be relocated as far as 6 feet from the old gas connection, if you plan to use the existing line. For new gas lines, you should hire a licensed plumber unless you're very well versed in gas installations. In any case, the work will require inspection by your building department before hookup.

Once your electrical or gas lines are in order, the actual hookup is straightforward.

Removing a range, oven, or cooktop. Before removing the old unit, first determine the method by which it is fastened (if it is fastened); for help, refer to the appropriate section on page 126. You'll probably need to unfasten some screws or clamps attaching the unit to the underside of the countertop, or to adjacent cabinets.

After removing the fasteners, move the appliance just far enough to gain access to the electrical or gas connection. If the appliance is electric, shut off the circuit to the appliance or appliance group before beginning the removal.

Gas appliances have individual shutoff valves (see drawing below). The valve is open when the handle is *parallel* to the pipe; to shut off the gas supply, turn the handle until it forms a *right angle* with the pipe. The appliance is connected to the shutoff valve and main gas line with either solid pipe or flexible tubing and compression fittings.

Solid pipe will need to be cut or unthreaded. A flexible connector can be removed from the shutoff valve with an adjustable wrench.

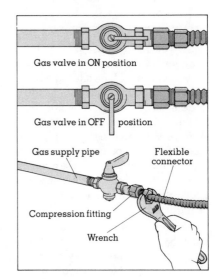

Gas valve in ON position

Gas valve in OFF position

Gas supply pipe

Flexible connector

Compression fitting

Wrench

Some gas appliances also have a 120-volt electrical connection that powers lights, timers, or thermostat. Unplug it or, if the connection is wired directly, shut off power to the circuit before disconnecting the wires.

If at any point you're unsure about how to proceed, call your utility company or seek other knowledgeable help.

Once both the fasteners and power connection are disassembled, the unit can be freely lifted or pulled out of position, loaded onto an appliance dolly, and transported from the room. Be sure you have adequate help for heavy jobs.

(Continued on next page)

... Fixtures & appliances

Installing a freestanding range. Except for the bulkiness of these units, this is a simple job to perform. Be sure the gas shutoff valve or electrical outlet is already in place. Slide the unit in part way until you can make the power hookup; then position it exactly. If the range has adjustable legs, raise or lower them to level the unit; otherwise, use shims as necessary.

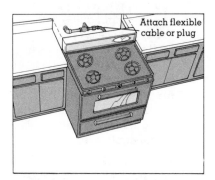

Attach flexible cable or plug

If you plan to use an existing gas connection, the new range must be within 6 feet of the shutoff valve. Check local gas or plumbing codes to determine if the connector may be flexible copper, brass, or aluminum, or if it must be solid pipe. A flexible connector is much simpler to install. Use an adjustable wrench to attach the connector's compression nuts to both range and shutoff as required.

Before turning the gas supply back on, it's wise to have utility company personnel check your work. They can inspect for gas leaks or air in the line, and can light and adjust the pilot lights on your new range.

Installing a drop-in range. This type of range is lowered into place between adjacent base cabinets. You'll need to determine the best method for attaching the power connection (either electric plug or gas connector) before, during, or after lifting the unit into place.

Some units have self-supporting flanges that sit on adjacent countertop surfaces. Others are simply lowered into place atop a special cabinet base. Fasten these ranges through side slots into the adjacent cabinets, or into the base itself. Bases and front trim that match

the surrounding cabinetry are available with many cabinet lines, or you can have them custom-made.

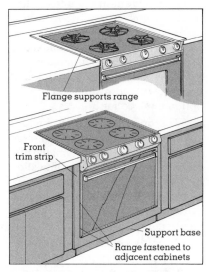

Flange supports range

Front trim strip

Support base

Range fastened to adjacent cabinets

Installing a cooktop. Standard electric and gas cooktops or combination cooktop-barbecue units are dropped into a countertop cutout, much as a new sink is installed (see page 121), then anchored from below with hardware supplied by the manufacturer. The power connection is in the cabinet directly below or to one side of the unit.

Electric cooktops may be plugged in or directly wired to a nearby junction box. A gas cooktop is normally connected by a flexible connector (check local codes), and must be located within 3 feet of its shutoff valve.

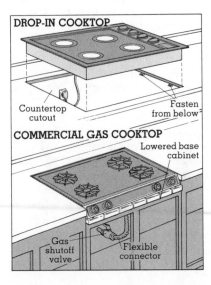

DROP-IN COOKTOP

Countertop cutout

Fasten from below

COMMERCIAL GAS COOKTOP

Lowered base cabinet

Gas shutoff valve

Flexible connector

Commercial gas cooktops sit on their own legs on the countertop. Often, a lowered base cabinet is used to align the cooktop with the surrounding countertop. Because of its resistance to heat, tile is frequently used below and surrounding the cooktop. The flexible gas connector is commonly run through a hole drilled in the countertop into the base cabinet below.

Many cooktops, especially those containing an indoor barbecue unit, have special downventing components that direct smoke, grease and moisture to a fan located in the base cabinet below. From that point, ducting runs out through the wall, or down through the cabinet base and below the floor.

Installing a wall oven. Separate wall ovens, either singly or in pairs, are housed in specially designed wall cabinets supplied in many sizes. Choose your wall oven first, and take the specifications with you when you shop for cabinets.

Wall ovens typically slide into place and rest atop support shelves. They're fastened to the cabinet through the sides or through overlapping flanges on the front. Trim strips are commonly available to fill any gaps between the ovens and the cabinet front.

The plug-in outlet or gas shutoff valve is usually located below the oven or ovens, inside the cabinet. If you plan both a microwave and a standard electric oven, you'll need both 120-volt and 120/240-volt outlets.

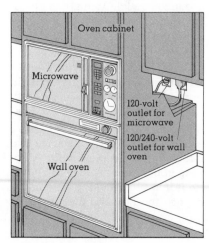

Oven cabinet

Microwave

120-volt outlet for microwave

120/240-volt outlet for wall oven

Wall oven

Installing a ventilation hood

The two basic types of ventilation hood are *ducted* and *ductless*. Though the ductless type is far easier to install (it requires no ductwork), the ducted version is far more efficient.

Before planning any ducting, or purchasing materials, check local mechanical codes for requirements.

Ducting basics. If you're simply replacing a ducted vent hood with a new one, you can probably use the old ducting to vent the new hood.

If you're starting from scratch, keep in mind that the straighter and shorter the path is from the hood to the outside, the more efficient the hood will be. Ducting can run either vertically through the roof or out through the wall, whichever is more direct and easier to install.

Ducting is available in both metal and plastic, and is either rectangular or round. The round type is available in both rigid and flexible varieties. The flexible type, though not as strong as the rigid sort, will follow a more twisted course without requiring fittings at each bend. However, if you use round ducting, you'll have to provide a transition fitting where the ducting meets the vent hood.

Join sections of ducting with duct tape. If any elbow fittings are re-

HOW TO MOUNT A VENT HOOD

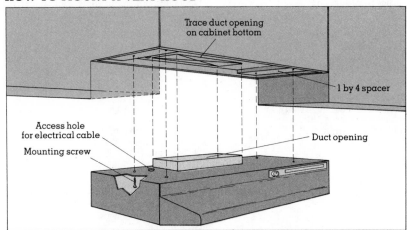

To mount a vent hood, trace the duct opening and electrical cable knockout hole on the wall cabinet or wall. Make the cutout with a drill and saber saw. If the cabinet bottom is recessed, add spacers to provide flush mounting surfaces.

quired, you'll need access to make the connection. Outside, protect the opening with either a flanged wall cap or a roof cap with integral flashing. Caulk around a wall cap to seal the seams between flange and siding. A roof cap's flashing must first be slipped under the roofing material; then all seams are liberally covered with roofing cement.

Mounting the hood. A vent hood is most commonly mounted on the bottom of an overhead wall cabinet. But first you must cut holes in the cabinet to correspond to knockout

holes on the vent's shell: one for the duct connector and one for the electrical cable.

Open the knockouts on the hood with a screwdriver and pliers. With a helper holding the hood flush with the front of the cabinet, trace the knockouts on the cabinet bottom. Drill out the electrical cable hole. Then drill pilot holes in the four corners of the duct connector outline, and cut out the area with a keyhole or saber saw.

The hood will mount to the bottom of the cabinet with screws provided; mark these spots next. If the cabinet's bottom is recessed, you'll have to add filler strips to attach the unit, as shown above. Then drill pilot holes for the screws. Adjusting the hood to fit perfectly flush with the cabinet front, fasten the hood to the cabinet. Thread the electrical cable through the appropriate cabinet hole, then through the knockout in the vent hood.

Hook up the electrical wires according to the manufacturer's instructions, making sure to attach the grounding screw to the grounding bracket on the hood.

Using duct tape or sheet metal screws, connect the vent hood's duct connector to the ducting inside the cabinet. Finally, install light bulbs, lighting panel, and filter panel.

TWO PATHS FOR A VENT DUCT

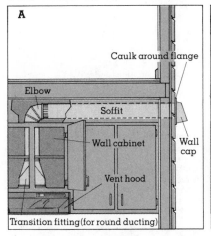

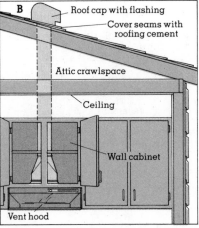

Two options for routing duct from a vent hood: run it horizontally in the space between wall cabinets and ceiling, or behind a soffit (A); or take the direct route up through the cabinet, ceiling, and attic to the roof (B).

Index

**Boldface numerals refer
to color photographs**

Appliances. *See also* names of individual
  appliances
  analyzing present, 18–19
  positioning in layout, 28–29
  styles and materials, 37–42
Architect, choosing, 46
Architectural symbols, 21

Building designer, choosing, 46
Building permits, obtaining, 45
Butcherblock, for countertops, **11,** 44, **53,
  62, 63, 70, 71, 73**

Cabinets, **74–79**
  analyzing present, 18
  planning, 31
  removing and installing, 108–109
  styles and materials, 43
  under-cabinet lighting, 102
Carpeting, **14,** 44
Ceiling
  analyzing present, 19
  raised, **3, 12, 14, 16**
  suspended, installing, 107
Ceramic tile
  countertops, 44, 112–113
  flooring, 44, 116–117
Color, in design, **6, 8,** 33, **49, 58, 61, 65**
Compactor
  installing, 125
  styles and materials, 42
Contractor, choosing, 46–47
Convection oven, 35, 38. *See also* Oven
Cooktop. *See also* Range
  analyzing present, 19
  energy conservation tips, 35
  removing and installing, 125–126
  styles and materials, 37
Cooling system, analyzing present, 19, 23
Costs, figuring, 45
Countertops, **60–63**
  analyzing present, 18
  heights of, 18, 24, 30–31
  installing, 111–113
  styles and materials, 44

Designer, choosing, 46–47
Design ideas, 48–**79**
  notebook for, 22
Design process, 24–34
Dimmer switches, 34
  installing, 101
Dishwasher
  analyzing present, 19
  energy conservation tips, 35
  removing and installing, 122–123
  styles and materials, 42
Disposer. *See* Garbage disposer
Door, hanging new, 86
Doorway
  closing off, **8,** 86–87
  framing new, 86

Eating area, **10, 16, 53, 55, 56, 59, 64, 75**
  analyzing present, 19
  locating, 19, 24–25, 29
Electrical outlets, 19, 94–97
Electrical system, basics, 93–97
Elevations, 20–21, 30–31
Energy conservation tips, 35

Faucet, removing and installing, 120–121
Financing, obtaining, 45
Fire prevention and control, 23
Flooring
  analyzing present, 19
  installing, 114–119
  styles and materials, 44
Floor plans, **8, 9, 11, 12, 13, 15,** 21, 26–27,
  30, 36, **50–53**
  measuring for and drawing, 20, 21, 30
Fluorescent lighting, 34
  installing, 98–102
Freezer
  analyzing present, 19
  energy conservation tips, 35
  styles and materials, 40

Garbage disposer
  removing and installing, 122
  styles and materials, 41
Gas system, working with, 92
Greenhouse
  addition, **13, 51, 64, 71**
  windows, **2, 7, 8,** 88

Hardwood floor. *See* Wood flooring
Heating system, analyzing present, 19, 23
Hood range
  installing, 127
  need for, 31
  styles and materials, 39
Hot water dispenser
  installing, 124
  styles and materials, 41

Icemaker, installing, 125
Incandescent lighting, 34
  installing, 98–102
Insurance, workers' compensation, 47

Layout. *See also* Floor plans
  analyzing present, 18
  constraints on new, 22–23
  designing new, 28–29
Lighting, **64–67**
  analyzing present, 19
  designing a lighting plan, 34
  fixtures, installing, 98–102
  recessed, **1, 3, 5, 9, 10, 13, 15,** 34, **50,
    53, 57, 58, 60, 64,** 100–101
  track, **13,** 34, **49, 60, 64,** 99–100
  under-cabinet, 102
Lines, in design, **8, 9,** 32, **49**

Makeovers, sample, **5–16**
Marble countertops, 44, 113
Microwave oven, 35, 38. *See also* Oven

Outlets, electrical, 19, 96, 97
Oven
  analyzing present, 19
  energy conservation tips, 35
  removing and installing, 125–126
  styles and materials, 38

Paint, using, 104–105
Permits, building, obtaining, 45
Planning guidelines, 16–47
Plans, floor, sample, 8, 9, 11, 12, 13, 15, 21,
  26–27, 30, 36
Plaster, patching, 110
Plastic laminate countertops, **8,** 44, **63, 74**
  installing, 111–112
Plumbing system, basics, 90–92

Radiant oven, 38. *See also* Oven
Range
  analyzing present, 19
  energy conservation tips, 35
  removing and installing, 125–126
  styles and materials, 39
Recessed lighting. *See* Lighting,
  recessed
Refrigerator
  analyzing present, 19
  energy conservation tips, 35
  removing and installing, 124–125
  styles and materials, 40
Remodeling basics, **80**–127
Resilient sheet flooring, **7,** 44, **55**
  installing, 114–115

Safety rules, 23, 24
Scale, considering, 32
Scale drawing, making, 20, 21, 30
Service rating, 94
Shapes, in design, 32, **49**
Sink
  analyzing present, 18
  complex, plumbing of, 90
  removing and installing, 121
  styles and materials, 41
Skylights, **3, 15, 64, 67, 80**
  installing, 89
  use in design, 34
Smoke detector, 23
Storage space, **74–79.** *See also* Cabinets
  analyzing present, 18
  planning for, 29, 31
Stove. *See* Range
Structural basics, 83–89
Subcontractors, hiring, 47
Surface-mounted lighting fixtures,
  installing, 98–99
Switches, wiring, 96–97

Tile countertops, 44
  installing, 112–113
Tile flooring, 44
  installing, 116–117
Traffic pattern, 18, 25, 27, 29
Trash compactor. *See* Compactor

Under-cabinet lighting, 102

Ventilation, analyzing present, 19
Ventilation hood. *See* Hood, range

Wallboard, gypsum
  installing, 103–104
  patching, 110
Wall oven. *See* Oven
Wallpaper, hanging, 105–107
Walls
  analyzing present, 19
  framing new, 84–85
  moving and removing, **9, 12, 15, 54, 55,**
    83–84
  patching, 110
Windows
  greenhouse, **2, 7, 8,** 88
  removing, framing, installing, 87
Wiring, electrical, 93–97
Wood flooring, 44
  installing and finishing, 117–119
Work centers, separating, 24, **68–73**
Workers, hiring, 47
Workers' compensation insurance, 47
Work surfaces. *See* Countertops
Work triangle, **8, 11, 12,** 18, 24, 28, **50, 51,
  53**